Maddalena Lombardini Sirmen

Eighteenth-Century Composer, Violinist, and Businesswoman

Elsie Arnold
Jane Baldauf-Berdes

The Scarecrow Press, Inc.
Lanham, Maryland, and London
2002

SCARECROW PRESS, INC.

Published in the United States of America
by Scarecrow Press, Inc.
A Member of the Rowman & Littlefield Publishing Group
4720 Boston Way, Lanham, Maryland 20706
www.scarecrowpress.com

4 Pleydell Gardens, Folkestone
Kent CT20 2DN, England

British Library Cataloguing in Publication Information Available

Library of Congress Cataloging-in-Publication Data

Arnold, Elsie.
   Maddalena Lombardini Sirmen : eighteenth-century composer, violinist, and
businesswoman / Elsie Arnold, Jane Baldauf-Berdes.
      p. cm.
   Includes bibliographical references (p.) and index.
   ISBN 0-8108-4107-X (alk. paper)
      1. Sirmen, Maddalena Laura Lombardini, 1745–1818. 2. Women
musicians—Italy—Venice—Biography. I. Berdes, Jane L. II. Title.

ML410.S594 A76 2002
780'.92—dc21
[B]   2001057703

⊖™ The paper used in this publication meets the minimum requirements of
American National Standard for Information Sciences—Permanence of
Paper for Printed Library Materials, ANSI/NISO Z39.48-1992.
Manufactured in the United States of America.

For our grandchildren:
Helen and Henry Arnold
Megan Willis and Renata Berdes

MADDALENA LOMBARDINI SIRMEN
with kind permission of the Civica Raccolta delle Stampe Achille Bertarelli, Castello Sforzesco, Milan

CONTENTS

ILLUSTRATIONS

ACKNOWLEDGMENTS

I should like to thank the following for their help and advice: Marie Thérèse Bouquet-Boyer, Gloria Eive, Giuseppe Ellero, Jonathan Glixon, Wendy Hancock, Patricia Howard, Simon McVeigh, John Arthur Smith, Kitty Southern, Michael Talbot, Gastone Vio, Micky White and Nigel Yandell. For help with translations: Madeleine Constable, Barbara Graziosi, and Kerstin Schofield; the following archives and libraries: Bergamo Misericordia Archive, Duke University Special Collection, Oxford Bodleian Library, London British Library, London Public Records Office, Ravenna Archivio Storico Communale and Biblioteca Classense, Rovigo Academia dei Concordi, Venice Archivio Patriarcale, Archivio di Stato and Istituzioni di Ricovero e di Educazione; and the following for permission for including extracts from their holdings and publications: Civica Raccolta delle Stampe Achille Bertarelli—Castello Sforzesco—Milano for the portrait of Sirmen, Macmillan Press Ltd for the extract from ed. Emily Anderson, *The Letters of Mozart and his Family*, the Moravian Music Foundation, and Yale University Beinecke Library. Above all I would like to thank George Berdes for encouraging me to write this book using much of the material brought to light by the painstaking researches of Jane. I am extremely grateful for the opportunity he has given me to learn more about this fascinating lady.

Elsie Arnold

READER'S NOTE

This information may assist the reader in understanding the period and place in which Sirmen lived.

Venetian Money Values

1739

1 zecchino	=	22 lire
1 ducato	=	6 lire 4 soldi
1 ducato di piazza	=	8 lire
1 ducatone	=	8 lire 18 soldi

Burney 1770

1 zecchino	=	22 lire, which was worth a little more than 9s English

Venetian Time

It is difficult to be accurate, since the day started at half an hour after sunset, the time of which differed throughout the year. In Venice, on January 1 the time of midday would be *c*. 19.09. I am grateful to Michael Talbot for this information which is fully explained in "*Ore Italiane*; The Reckoning of the Time of Day in pre-Napoleonic Italy" (*Italian Studies* [1985], 51–62).

INTRODUCTION

The rediscovery of the life and music of Maddalena Laura Lombardini Sirmen is almost entirely due to the painstaking and diligent researches of Jane Baldauf-Berdes. Jane's master's thesis was on the subject of Maddalena's *Six Violin Concertos*, and it was accepted by the University of Maryland in 1979. The research needed to write this thesis obviously fired Jane's imagination and since Maddalena Lombardini Sirmen had been a pupil at the *Ospedale dei Mendicanti*, Jane became interested in the whole history of the Venetian *ospedali*. She was an unstoppable researcher and discovered an incredible amount of new information about the Venetian *ospedali*. She was greatly helped—as indeed I have been myself over the years—by the immense kindness and generosity of Dr Giuseppe Ellero of the *Istituzioni di Ricovero e di Educazione di Venezia*, where some of the archives of the Mendicanti are stored, and the distinguished archivist Don Gastone Vio, who has devoted many years to archival research. For information about Ravenna, and Maddalena's husband, Lodovico, Dr Gaetano Ravaldini was generous with his time and the material he found concerning the Sirmens.

Jane then decided to become a research student in the Faculty of Music of the University of Oxford, where she was supervised by my late husband, Denis Arnold. He, alas, died before her thesis was completed and she gained her doctorate in 1989 with a thesis entitled *Musical Life at the Four Ospedali Grandi of Venice, 1525–1855*. This was the basis of her book *Women Musicians of Venice: Musical Foundations, 1515–1855* (Clarendon Press, Oxford 1993). Sadly, Jane developed cancer, and when she knew she was unlikely to recover, she asked me to take on the task of bringing Maddalena's music and life to a wider audience. With great humility I agreed, and Jane's husband, George, generously allowed me access to her research material, which is now housed in the Special Collections Library of Duke University, North Carolina.

Until recently Maddalena Lombardini Sirmen was regarded mainly as a violin pupil of Tartini and the recipient of a letter from him in which he explains his teaching methods, how to practise, and how to create beautiful sounds from the instrument. Not that Maddalena's name ever entirely disappeared from our music encyclopaedias and dictionaries, but in them she is barely discussed as a composer in her own right, simply as Tartini's pupil. But we now have a much broader view of this extraordinary lady: how she managed her own life, her concert engagements, and her finances. She was certainly an excellent business woman.

So this is the reason the book has two authors. Much of the documentary evidence from Italy was collected by Jane, but the writing—except where stated—is all mine, so I take full responsibility for any errors. But I must confess I have so much enjoyed discovering the life and times of this remarkable lady that I shall be eternally grateful to Jane for giving me this opportunity.

Elsie Arnold

ABBREVIATIONS

ACP   Venice, Curia Patriarcale

AP   Venice, Archivio Patriarcale

Arte   Ed. Giuseppe Ellero, Jolando Scarpa, Maria Carla Paolucci, *Arte e Musica all'Ospedaletto* (Venice, 1978)

Bouquet   Bouquet, Marie-Thérèse, *Il Teatro di Corte dalle Origini al 1788* (Turin: Cassa di Risparmio, 1976)

Fabbri   Paolo Fabbri, *Tre Secoli di Musica a Ravenna* (Ravenna, 1983)

Germany   Burney, *The Present State of Music in Germany, the Netherlands, and the United Provinces* (London, 1775)

Ghiselli   Ghiselli, I. Gamba: *De fatti di Ravenna*, 15 vols. in the *Archivio Storico Communale di Ravenna*, mss RAasc Gamba n. 65.

History   Burney, *A General History of Music from the Earliest Ages to the Present Period. To which is prefixed a Dissertation on the Music of the Ancients* (London, 1776, 1782, 1789). Mod. reprint ed. F. Mercer (New York, 1957)

IRE   Venice, Istitutzioni di Ricovero e di Educazione

MV   *More Veneto.* The Venetian year began on 1 March, so dates in January and February refer to the previous year

OLP   *Ospedali e Luoghi Pii Diversi*, catalogue section in the Archivio di Stato, Venice

PA	*Public Advertiser*
Pierre	C. Pierre, *Histoire du Concert Spirituel, 1725–90* (Paris, 1900)
Poole	Ed. E.H. Poole, *Charles Burney: Music, Men, and Manners in France and Italy, 1770* (London: Folio Society, 1969)
Stone	G.W. Stone, *The London Stage, 1660–1800* (Carbondale, Ill. 1952), vol. III, part 4, 1747–1776
Scholes	Percy A. Scholes, *The Great Dr Burney*, 2 vols. (London: Oxford University Press, 1948)
Tour	Burney, *The Present State of Music in France and Italy, or the Journal of a tour through those countries, undertaken to collect Materials for a General History of Music,* London, printed for T. Becket & Co. in the Strand (1771, 1773) modern edition, ed. P. Scholes (Oxford, 1959)
VAS	Venice, Archivio di Stato

The library sigla are those used in *The New Grove Dictionary of Music and Musicians* (London: Macmillan, 1980).

Chapter 1

BACKGROUND

Count Czernin is not content with fiddling at Court, and as
he would like to do some conducting, he has collected an
amateur orchestra who are to meet in Count Lodron's hall
every Sunday after three o'clock . . . After the symphony
Count Czernin played a beautifully written concerto by
Sirmen.[1] (The complete extract from the letter is included
in Appendix A)

On 12 April 1778, Leopold Mozart, Wolfgang's father, wrote this in a
letter from Salzburg to his wife and son in Paris. If he had been writing
today he might easily have said "a beautifully written concerto by the
woman composer Sirmen", but no, her sex was of no interest. So,
although Maddalena Laura Lombardini Sirmen has been almost forgotten for over a hundred and fifty years, during her lifetime she was an
international figure, famous as composer, violinist, and singer and not
just as an unusual woman able to do these things. Copies of her music
can still be found in collections as far apart as Finland, Naples, and
Winston-Salem in the United States.

Maddalena Laura Lombardini was born in Venice in 1745; women
composers were not unknown there. After the Venetian songwriter
Barbara Strozzi (1619–after 1664), came Marietta Giusti, the daughter
of the organist Paolo Giusti, who was a pupil of Andrea Gabrieli.

Marietta was among the earliest music teachers at the *Ospedale dei Mendicanti*, where Maddalena was to be educated. Anna Boni (*c.* 1738–?), the daughter of the Bolognese artist Girolamo Boni, was educated in Venice at the *Ospedale della Pietà*, and since she had a surname, was not a foundling but a fee-paying pupil. Her earliest published music was printed in Nuremberg in 1756 when she was "Virtuosa di Musica di Camera" to Frederick the Great.

Maddalena's family members, however, were not professional musicians, neither members of the aristocracy nor the church; she had to make her own way in a very masculine world, and we must admire her for her determination, business ability—she made a lot of money— and dedication to her profession. So why has she been forgotten? The music written in the eighteenth century was not on the whole enjoyed by the nineteenth, and it was not until the twentieth century that composers such as Vivaldi were rediscovered and began to be appreciated. So it was with Maddalena.

In many ways she was fortunate in having been born in Venice. From the fifteenth century onward, to the rest of the world Venice appeared a model of stability. She was a republic (no wars of succession), had survived the hostilities of the previous centuries, and appeared impregnable. As the Englishman Edward Wright wrote:

> 'Tis a pleasure, not without a Mixture of Surprise, to
> see so great a City as Venice may truly be call'd, as it
> were, floating on the Surface of the Sea, to see
> Chimneys and Towers, where you could expect
> nothing but Ship-Masts. It stands surrounded with
> Waters, at least five Miles distant from any Land; and
> is thus defended by its fluid Bulwark better than by
> Walls or ramparts; for, let the Venetians but pluck up
> their Poles out of the Lagune, and they may defy any
> foreign Vessels coming near them by Water; and by
> Land there's no coming at them.[2]

During the sixteenth and early seventeenth centuries, the tourists were urged to visit St Mark's church. Here was the Westminster Abbey of the Venetian Republic. It was not the cathedral—that was the church of S. Pietro di Castello—but the Doge's own Chapel. In effect it was the state church and over the centuries had built up an impressive number of ceremonies and customs. As Francesco Sansovino in his magnificent *Venetia Città Nobilissima et Singolare* said ". . . the income for each year is more than 12 thousand ducats, which provides for two well-paid organists, the best in Italy, the *maestro di capella* (in charge of the music) and a good number of singers".[3] Then times changed. During the brilliant years of Andrea Gabrieli (1533–*c*. 1586), Giovanni Gabrieli (*c*. 1555–1612), and Claudio Monteverdi (1567–1643), the choir and orchestra of St Mark's were outstanding. Then came opera. The first public opera house opened in Venice in 1637. The singers became popular figures and could command high fees, so the best singers in the churches left to become opera stars. The pay was much better in the opera houses. The composers also seem to us not to have the genius of their predecessors, and they too spent much of their time composing operas.

In 1697 Vincenzo Coronelli began publishing a series of guide books for foreign visitors to Venice, *Guida de' Forestieri Sacro-Profana per osservare il più Ragguardevole nella Città di Venezia*. It was the equivalent of one of our present-day guides, included a plan of the city and was full of useful information. Regarding music, in the 1706 edition, he recommended visits to the chapels of the *ospedali*.

> The [singers and instrumentalists] among the *figlie* [literally "daughters"] of the four *ospedali* are very celebrated. The famous Cecilia, Apollonia, and Coccina sing at the Incurabili; Vienna, Cecilia, Antonina, and la Turchetta at the Mendicanti, where Barbara plays the organ and oboe extremely well; at the Ospedaletto there is the celebrated singer la Vicentina and at the Pietà la Jamosa plays the archlute.

The *ospedali* were charitable institutions; Venice was proud of them. They had a mixture of purposes—that of hospital for the sick and elderly, orphanage, and home for the poor. The oldest was the *Ospedale di S. Lazzaro e dei Mendicanti*, founded around 1182 as an asylum for lepers, the destitute, and crusaders; then followed the *Ospedale degl'Incurabili* to treat syphilis, the *Ospedale di Santa Maria dei Derelitti* (or *Ospedaletto*) for orphans, beggars, and the sick, and, finally, the *Ospedale della Pietà* as a refuge for unwanted babies. Thomas Coryat, who visited Venice for six weeks in 1608, wrote:

> In the south wall of which building that looketh towards the sea, I observed a certaine yron grate insert-

ed into a hollow peece of the wall, betwixt which grate
and a plaine stone beneath it, there is a convenient little
space to put in an infant. Hither doth the mother or
some body for her bring the child shortly after it is
borne into the world; and if the body of it be no greater,
but that it may be conveniently without any hurt to the
infant bee conveighed in at the foresaid space, they put
it in there.[4]

The English merchant Robert Bargrave arrived in Venice 16 April
1655. He was well educated, a musician—he played the viol—and
poet. He had written a masque on the marriage of two of his friends,
the unfortunate first line being "Thou rude unpolished Lump". In
Majorca he enjoyed "their cathedral mussique . . . with nuns voices and
a great variety of instruments" and spent five years in Turkey. In
Venice he wrote:

> and lastly their Musick, which is indeed generally
> excellent, whether privat or publique: yet is surpassed
> in the two Nunneries of Beggars [the Mendicanti] and
> the Bastards [the Pietà]. . . Lastly in expressing of
> words by singing according to theyr sence: as *Morire*
> dolefully, *Sospiri* sighingly, and *Ridendo* laughingly.[5]

And it was at the *Ospedale dei Mendicanti* that Maddalena received her
musical and general education; from the age of seven she was to spend
fourteen years there.

All the *ospedali* catered for both sexes with strict segregation in the
buildings. The young men left when quite young; they were taught a
trade and many went into the navy. The young women stayed until they
were older; the institutions could hardly have sent them into the streets,
so they too were taught how to make a living and when they left were
given dowries. Sometime in the seventeenth century the music in the
chapels became increasingly important. The *ospedali*, like charitable
institutions today, were always short of money. It was then realized
that easy-to-listen-to music, well performed by a female choir and
instrumentalists, brought in the crowds—and the money. Since the girls
remained longer in the *ospedali* than the boys, it was from them that
the potential musicians were found. Girls who showed musical ability
were taught by the best teachers that could be found for them in
Venice. The music in the chapels of the *ospedali* became famous, and

they were soon on the tourist route.[6] There are many surviving accounts by visitors of services in the chapels of the *ospedali*; here is a typical one from a later date:

> In these conservatories, of which some aged senators take on themselves the management, female orphans or foundlings are maintained, brought up under the best masters, and portioned; each of these foundations being very plentifully endowed. The tendency of the education, however, seems rather to make Laises and Aspasias [learned women], than nuns or mothers of families, and the capital part of it is music. These conservatories have alternatively vespers in music, very finely performed, and concluding with a grand motet, which is sold by women who let chairs to sit on; the words are nothing but a most wretched uncouth jumble of Latin phrases in rhyme, and stuffed rather with barbarisms and solecisms, than any thing of sense and propriety; indeed the author is generally the sexton. On this paltry ground, however, is wrought the most delicate music, of which both the vocal and instrumental parts are performed only by the girls of the house (whom you see through the grate, which is hung with a very slight crape) fluttering about and throwing themselves into all the attitudes required in the execution of the most spirited music.[7]

The Venetians enjoyed the music too. Here is an excerpt from a contemporary journal for July 1687:

> In this Seminary [the Mendicanti] of little angel singers there are some forty girls who are training to be used in the *coro* [musical establishment]. Some of these young artists can sing and play, as well, on every kind of musical instrument. And they do so with such expertise that they are without equals even among secular musicians. The Apollo for this Parnassus is the Very Excellent Doctor Domenico Partenio, who is also *vice-maestro di cappella* at the Doge's Chapel of St Mark. He is so skilled a composer that when his works are joined by the sweetness of these voices from Paradise, they become a choir of Seraphims. [Signora Maria Anna Ziani] sang a solo motet and did so with the

ultimate in musicianship. Even though she is a woman,
Signora Ziani possesses the baritone voice that is quite
masculine sounding, though still with qualities of
tenderness and fullness. . . . In addition to being a
particularly fine singer, this very same lady plays the
violin with such openness and melodic intensity that I
dare say, if Euridice had only possessed half so
excellent skills, her Orfeo would never have had to
descend into Hell in an attempt to free her from the
internal jaws.[8]

Notes

1. Emily Anderson, ed., *The Letters of Mozart and his Family* (London: Macmillan, 1985), 526–27.

2. Edward Wright, *Some Observations made in Travelling through France, Italy &c in the Years 1720, 1721 and 1722* (London, 1730), 45.

3. (Venice, 1663), 104.

4. Thomas Coryat, *Coryat's Crudities* (London, 1611), I, 381–83.

5. Oxford Bodleian Library Rawlinson mss C799 fol. 162–63.

6. For a full history of the *ospedali* see Jane Baldauf-Berdes, *Women Musicians of Venice: Musical Foundations 1525–1855* (Oxford: Clarendon Press, 1993, rev. ed. 1996).

7. Thomas Nugent, tr., *New Observations on Italy and its Inhabitants: Written in French by Two Swedish Gentlemen* (London, 1769), 264.

8. *Pallade Veneta*, July 1687, 58–62.

Chapter 2

CHILDHOOD

We know little of Maddalena's family background. Her mother was baptised in the church of S. Raffaele Arcangelo, Venice, on 10 June 1714:

> Gasparina Iseppa, daughter of Signor Antonio, a barber, son of late Gaudentio Gambirasi and his legal wife Anna Maria, daughter of the late Zuanne Tandina, was born on the third of June. Iseppo Gagieta is godfather, the midwife was La Tognella both of our neighbourhood.[1]

It is interesting to see that Maddalena's maternal grandfather was a barber; perhaps her musical genius came from him. Barbers were often musicians; for example Antonio Vivaldi's father, Giovanni Battista, was a barber as well as a professional violinist. The marriage contract of 4 September 1740 between Maddalena's father, Piero, and her mother states:

> A marriage contract has been negotiated between Piero, son of Sebastian Lombardini, widower of Zuanna Folin, and Gasparina Gambirasi, daughter of Signor Antonio Gambirasi, both of our neighbourhood, he lives in Calle dello Squero, she near Cà Barbarigo.[2]

The marriage took place on 2 October 1740:

> Permission having been granted, the above-mentioned
> Sebastian and Gasparina were joined in holy matrimony by
> exchanging vows. They received the nuptual blessings
> from me, Father Francesco Fontana, incumbent and sacris-
> tan of the church of S. Sebastiano. In the presence of
> Domenico Bartoli, son of the late Giovanni Maria Bartoli,
> who lives in the parish of S. Basilio and our parish clerk,
> Agostin Baggin.[3]

A mistake seems to have been made in this document, since the
husband's name was Piero, which is used correctly in the notice of
their forthcoming marriage. After the wedding they probably settled
down in the Calle dello Squero—since demolished—off the Campo di
S. Angelo in Dorsoduro, which had been Piero's home. Their first
child, Angela, married Francesco Gottardi in 1762, and the marriage
document shows that Piero Lombardini had died by then, although the
family still lived in Campo S. Angelo. Maddalena was born five years
after the wedding on 9 December 1745:

> Campo dell'Angelo. Maddalena Laura, daughter of Signor
> Piero Lombardini, son of the late Sebastian Lombardini,
> and Piero's lawful wife, Signora Gasparina Gambirasi
> Lombardini, daughter of Antonio Gambirasi, was born on 9
> December. The godfather is Iseppo, son of the late
> Domenico Furlanetto of the parish of S. Nicolò. The
> midwife was Orsola Basso. She was baptised by the
> incumbent Signor Fogliarolo.[4]

There is something strange about the entry of Maddalena's date of birth
in the church records. At first it looks as though the date should be
1750, but closer examination (by Jane Baldauf-Berdes) shows that the
correct date is 1745. Why this happened is a mystery. We know
nothing further about Maddalena's childhood until her attempt in 1753
to enter the *Ospedale dei Mendicanti* as a potential musician.

After its foundation around 1182, the Mendicanti moved several
times. Eventually in 1595 a new building was planned between the
Fondamenta Nuove and the church and Campo of SS Giovanni e Paolo
to house four hundred adults and one hundred children. The original
buildings are still used and are the nucleus of the present *Ospedale
Civile*. The main entrance leads from the Fondamenta dei Mendicanti
through an impressive entrance hall to the chapel beyond. There you

THE MENDICANTI IN THE EIGHTEENTH CENTURY
with kind permission of the Bodleian Library, Oxford (ref. Vet.F.4.a.1)

can still see the galleries with their lovely wrought iron fronts, behind which the girls performed. The structure is in the form of a double monastery, the women's part on the right as you enter from the canal, the men's on the left. Each had its own cloister and garden with a well in the centre and seems almost self-contained. There was a room for the porter, one which had its own entrance leading onto the street, which could be turned into a shop for selling cloth, a store of material to put out fires, storage rooms for flour, wine, wood, rooms for the sick, the children's nurse and her assistant, kitchens, refectories, a dispensary for medicines, a shoemaker, a room for the priest, and many more.

Musical activity for women in the Mendicanti started in a very modest way. In 1604 eight girls from the *Ospedale* were chosen to sing the offices to join the four who were already doing this. This expansion continued between 1605 and 1609, when extra girls came from the Zitelle, another orphanage on the Giudecca, to sing three times a week for twenty ducats a year. In 1616 Marietta Giusti, organist, teacher, composer, and daughter of the organist Paolo Giusti—a pupil of Andrea Gabrieli and second organist at St Mark's—was employed by the Mendicanti to teach the girls and to maintain discipline since there had been "grave disorders" among the singers. She had previously been in the musical establishment of the Pietà, and was now paid twelve ducats a year to include board, lodging, and uniform. If, however, she left the post, her father would have to return any money spent on her. Incidentally, the Zitelle had to close in 1619 because of a *humor malinconico*.

There must have been some musical instruments for the chapel since, except for the organ, they were abolished in 1619; however, they gradually crept back. In 1639 the first *musico* was appointed— Giovanni Rovetta—and the Mendicanti bought "good violins to be played in the choir".[5] By 1661 they owned two portative organs, one spinetta, two clavichords, three trombones, one violin, one violetta, one viola da braccio, two violinos, one bassoon, and one theorbo, and by 1683 they owned in all about forty instruments.

A *Priora* was the head of the female part of the Mendicanti. Later, in 1767 (MV 1768), the year Maddalena left to get married, there were eleven members of staff: a doctor (*medico*), surgeon (*chiurgico*), pharmacist (*spezier*), an administrative assistant (*fattor*), bookkeeper

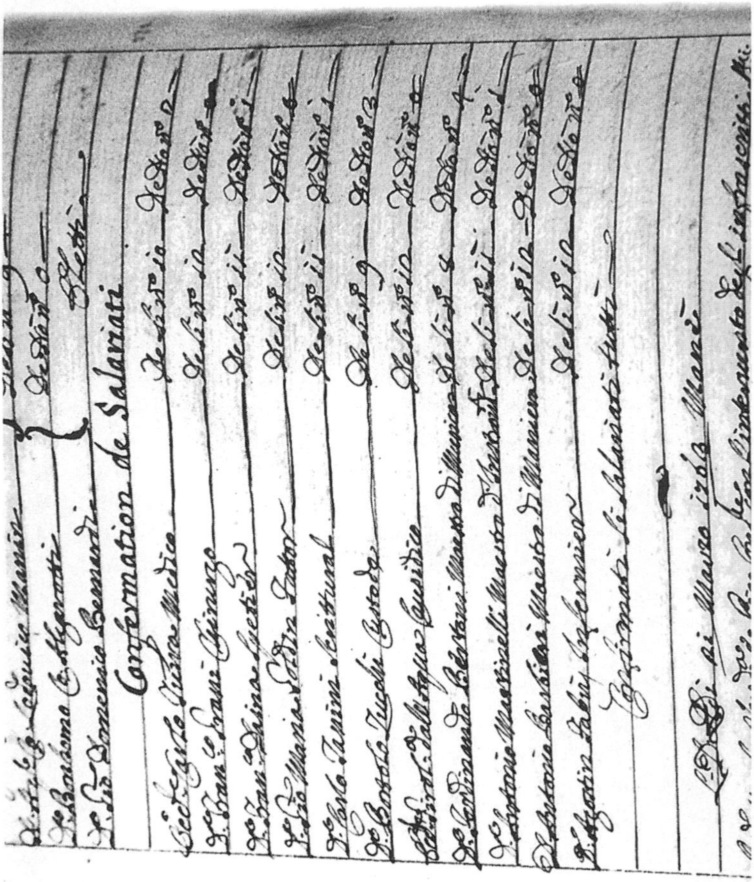

SALARIES AT THE MENDICANTI IN 1767

(*scritturale*), head of the women's hospital (*infermier*), warden (*custode*), and legal advisor (*causidico*). There are receipts for some of their salaries. In 1763: *medico* 12 ducats 12 grossi; *chiurgico* 6 ducats 6 grossi; *infermier* 6½ ducats, all for three months; *spezier* 75 ducats for six months.[6] There were three musicians: a *maestra di coro, di strumenti*, and *di maniera*. There was also a woman *maestra di coro* from one of the mature members of the choir. Her duties were quite onerous: she had to take her orders from the governing body, keep the beat (conduct), intone the responses, deliver the readings during the divine office, and look after all other aspects of the life of the *figlie* whether they were members of the *coro* or not.[7]

The Mendicanti employed some distinguished musicians such as Giovanni Legrenzi (1626–90), *maestro di coro* 1676–82; Giovanni Battista Vivaldi (1655–1736), father of Antonio, *maestro di strumenti* 1689–93; Baldassare Galuppi (1706–85), *maestro di coro* 1740–51 who rather disgraced himself by leaving Venice for London to compose operas; and, finally, Ferdinando Bertoni (1725–1813), *maestro di coro* 1752–97. This investment in good musicians paid off and gradually the money from music, both from performances in the chapel and for private occasions, became useful to the finances of the *Ospedale*. The larger the congregations, the more money came from hiring the *scagni*, or chairs, more teachers were employed, and music copyists employed. The governors of the *ospedali* had much in common with the trustees of charities today; money raising was of prime importance. When a will was being made, the notary had to suggest that a portion of the person's estate should be given to charity. Many people left money so that masses could be said for their souls after death; every *ospedale* had priests on its staff (*mansionari*) to say these masses.

The *maestri di cori* were composers who were expected to write music for their employers; by the early eighteenth century, music had become big business. To raise the standard of performance, girls with special musical ability began to be admitted to the *ospedali*, even though they were not orphans, and eventually the music teaching became so well known that girls were sent from some distance as boarders to receive a good education, a general as well as a musical one. For example, the King of Poland in 1730 asked permission to send two sisters, Anna and Rosa Negri, to be trained at the Pietà.[8] So, the Venetian *ospedali* became the first music schools for women. And how everybody loved them! In June 1739 the French lawyer and scholar Charles de Brosses wrote to his friend M. de Blancey:

> The best music is that of the asylums. There are four of them, made up of illegitimate and orphaned girls whose parents are not in a position to raise them . . . they sing like angels and play the violin, flute, organ, oboe, cello and the bassoon; in short, there is no instrument, however unwieldy, that can frighten them . . . I vow to you that there is nothing so diverting as the sight of a young pretty nun in white habit, with a bunch of pomegranate blossoms over her ear, conducting the orchestra and beating time with all the grace and precision imaginable.[9]

De Brosses had got it slightly wrong; the performers were not nuns.

In 1753 there was a musical crisis in the Mendicanti: on 28 July the members of the governing board agreed the following:

> and since the number of our *figlie* has dropped to 60 from the end of 1748 we suggest it should be increased to 70 and that as now there are 64 members of the *coro* 6 new girls will be admitted between the ages of 6 and 8 . . . Bearing in mind the above-discussed lack of organists, the selection committee is advised that if a promising young organist is among the new applicants, she should be given every opportunity to develop her skill . . . The new *figlie* will accompany funerals, and be given the necessary educational opportunities.[10]

Two months later, on 21 September the auditions took place, and Maddalena was one of the thirty girls trying for entrance. It must have been a tremendous ordeal for a child of seven to be auditioned by about thirty-three people. One wonders what they were asked to do. At the first ballot there were three girls with outstanding marks who were immediately accepted: Maria Isabetta Emilia Terri, 31 for, 2 against; Christina Lelia Terri, 27 for, 6 against; and Lucrezia Elizabetta Semenzi, 19 for, 14 against. On this ballot Maddalena gained 18 for and 15 against. On the second ballot she again gained 18 for and 15 against and was accepted.[11]

What sort of life was ahead for her? To us, the restrictions sound formidable. Their parents and siblings could visit once a month, uncles, aunts, and cousins, every three months, and a member of staff had to be present during these visits. Presents, messages, and letters should first be opened by the *Signora Priora*, and the rules for the musicians had to be explained to them when they were accepted. The *coro* was divided into three groups:

  (i)   Beginners (*incipienti*), until age 16.
  (ii) The second (*proficienti*) for advanced students, for 5 years.
  (iii) The third (*essercitanti*) for professionals, members must remain in this group for 10 years.

> When passing from one group to another, or when promotion does not seem advisable and a *figlia* remains in the same group for longer than is required, administrators must take care to determine whether a *figlia's* intention is to leave the *coro* or not. In the case of professionals (*essercitanti*) none can leave until they have taught two others to take their places. After these 10 years they can marry or become nuns. Those wishing to marry are to be given double [the dowry] of those who enter the religious life.[12]

It was not "all work and no play" however, as Madeleine Constable discovered:[13]

> . . . an anonymous manuscript poem of 39 stanzas entitled "carnevale per le putte de" Mendicanti in stile bernesco' and bearing the date 1750. This burlesque in Venetian dialect tells of the endeavours of the *figlie del coro* at the Mendicanti to provide by their own extempore musical efforts some measure of compensation within the walls of their *pio luogo* for the unwelcome fact that they were not allowed to participate in the jollifications of Carnival . . . The opening stanzas describe the girls' attitude to what seems to them a state of imprisonment, and then come several stanzas describing the Carnival celebrations. This preamble leads to the choristers' own contribution to the general merriment, their improvised concert. If the girls still feel able, with some touches of irony, to sing the praises of those in authority over them, seen collectively, they are more discriminating over particular individuals more closely affecting their lives . . . [for] the *Priora* . . . the motivation behind the daily discipline . . . is love or charity, which is yet hardly apparent in practice. The resident Somaschian priest, however, is referred to in complimentary terms as a devoted pastor, a welcome figure of

authority and one showing no favouritism . . . [for Galuppi]
the praise is wholehearted, both for the much loved teacher
and for the musician of whose merits the choristers are well
aware. After a further stanza proclaiming the merits of their
mistresses in which they pay tribute to their kindness and
patience (whether with irony or true gratitude is not clear),
the choristers, in a final outburst of benevolence, toast the
entire community and its benefactors and also the girls of
the Mendicanti past and present, bestowing their good
wishes to those who leave to follow the dictates of their
hearts.

As soon as Maddalena had been accepted into the Mendicanti's
coro, she was given Chiara Variati as her "mother substitute" or *zia
d'educazione*, and from then on would wear the uniform dress of black
serge with a high neck and fitted bodice. There is an entry in the
Mendicanti archive for 2 February 1679:

Having been made aware of the great indecency of the
dress of the *figlie del coro*, who adorn themselves to their
own liking, thus undesirably stimulating further licen-
tiousness, it is resolved that they all be clothed by the same
dressmaker, to be appointed by the governors, in woollen
cloth of a dark colour. The same to apply to shoes.[14]

But they did wear pretty collars for their performances.

We do not know whether Maddalena played any instruments when
she was admitted, but if not, she soon would. The girls worked hard.
They studied the fundamentals of music: sight-singing (*cantare a
prima vista*), ear training, performance practice (*maniera*) and counter-
point/composition. From the *maestro d'istrumenti* they learned to play
all the instruments which the *Ospedale* owned and were given
excellent voice training which included trills and rapid scales
(*passaggi*). They were also given a good general education. The school
was staffed by Somaschian priests, a teaching order, and the
curriculum included Greek, Latin, grammar, poetry, logic, history, and
French. But they had only one day of holiday each year when they
often went to one of the islands for a picnic. On performance days they
got extra food—meat to the value of ½ lira, and the days before that
fish to the value of 4 soldi.

Ferdinando Bertoni had been made *maestro di coro e di musica* in
1752. He had taken over from Baldassare Galuppi, whose dealings

with the Mendicandi were rather chequered to say the least of it. Galuppi was appointed *maestro di coro* in 1740 at a salary of 250 ducats initially for three years. But the following year we find him asking the Governors for leave:

> I have been asked by several English gentlemen, lovers of music, to take part in some of their activities . . . I have written no fewer than 31 compositions for the choir in the course of a year . . . what must move the pious spirits of Your Excellencies . . . is the state of my numerous and poor family of no fewer than twelve persons, of whom seven are of marriageable age, for whom I must find from heaven their bread and daily sustenance.[15]

Galuppi actually stayed in London for two years and the "lovers of music" were the management of the King's Theatre in the Haymarket who were probably offering Galuppi a generous fee. However, it was during his time at the Mendicanti that the music school really began to flourish. The Governors raised his salary by 100 ducats in 1744 because "the choir has become not inferior to any other but in truth can be said to have become distinctly praiseworthy", [16] and on the same day agreed to enlarge the choir gallery (*cantoria*) "since it was too small to take the 80 girls of the choir" including "those who understand well how to play instruments". The performers could not even all see the *maestro di coro*. By September the work was nearly complete, and "the enlarging of the *cantoria* has made it much more convenient to all the girls who serve in the choir: the instruments can be played fully and conveniently, and the voices can now be placed at best advantage . . .".[17] Then Galuppi got caught up in the world of opera, his famous collaboration with Goldoni was in full swing, and by 1751 he had no time for the Mendicanti. The minute book records in 1752:

> Since we have been without a *maestro di coro* since 30 November of last year, the members of the choir present Ferdinando Bertoni, whose compositions have been performed with success during Lent. He is elected *maestro di coro e di musica* with all the obligations of his predecessor. He will receive a salary of 250 ducats per annum.[18]

And it was Bertoni who was in charge of the music throughout Maddalena's time at the Mendicanti. He was still there in 1777, after which the record books have disappeared. Ferdinando Bertoni (1725–

1813) was born at Salò on Lake Garda, which was then Venetian
territory. After studying with Padre Martini in Bologna, he settled in
Venice in 1745 as organist of the church of S. Moisè, soon writing an
opera for the Theatre S. Cassiano and two oratorios for the church of S.
Maria di Consolatione, usually known as the Fava. He visited London
1778–80 and 1781–83 as conductor and opera composer. Charles
Burney in his *A General History of Music* (London, 1776–89) gives
one of his all-too-common lukewarm descriptions of musicians he
knew:

> Though the invention of this master is not very fertile, his
> melody is graceful and interesting; and though he never
> had perhaps sufficient genius and fire to attain the sublime,
> yet he is constantly natural, correct, and judicious; often
> pleasing and sometimes happy.[19]

Unfortunately we have not so far found a description of Bertoni
written by one of his Venetian musicians, but do have an anecdote
from Mrs Piozzi who had formerly been Mrs Thrale and a friend of Dr
Johnson. She visited Italy with her second husband, Gabriel Piozzi, and
while in Venice in 1785 wrote:

> The famous Ferdinand Bertoni, so well known in London
> for his long residence among us, and from the undisputed
> merit of his compositions, now inhabits this his native city,
> and being fond of *dumb creatures*, as we call them, took to
> petting a pigeon . . . This creature has, by keeping his
> master company, I trust, obtained so perfect an ear and
> taste for music that no one who sees his behaviour, can
> doubt for a moment the pleasure he takes in hearing Mr
> Bertoni play and sing, for as soon as he sits down to the
> instrument, Columbo begins shaking his wings, perches on
> the piano-forte, and expresses the most indubitable
> emotions of delight. If, however, he or anyone strike a note
> false, or make any kind of discord upon the keys, the dove
> never fails to show evident tokens of anger and distress;
> and if teized too long, grows quite enraged; pecking the
> offenders legs and fingers in such a manner, as to leave
> nothing less doubtful than the sincerity of his resentment.[20]

As an antidote to Burney's evaluation of Bertoni's music, Gerald
Larner, when reviewing Bertoni's *Orfeo* performed in Monte Carlo in
May 1995, wrote in *The Times* of London on 23 May:

Ferdinando Bertoni's *Orfeo* is uncommonly interesting. Written for Gaetano Guadagni, Gluck's first Orfeo, it is the singer's answer to reformed opera, offering a succession of shamelessly decorative display arias for Orfeo and one or two for Euridice and Imeneo as well. It does so so effectively that it was customary until quite recently— Marilyn Horne insisted on it—for singers to violate the chastity of Gluck's *Orfeo* by inserting Bertoni arias.

Charles Burney was in Venice in 1770. Many visitors to Venice wrote accounts of visiting the *ospedali*, but since Burney was a professional musician, his depths of musical knowledge make his descriptions especially interesting. He was there in August and although Maddalena had left the Mendicanti in 1767, it is doubtful whether much would have changed in three years:

> In the afternoon of the same day I went to the hospital *de'Mendicanti*, for orphan girls, who are taught to sing and play, and on Sundays and festivals they sing divine service in chorus. Signor Bertoni is the present *Maestro di Capella*. There was a hymn performed with solo and choruses, and a *mottetto a voce sola*, which last was very well performed, particularly an accompanied recitative, which was pronounced with great force and energy. Upon the whole, the compositions had some pretty passages, mixed with others that were not new. The subjects of the fugues and choruses were trite and slightly put together. The girls here I thought accompanied the voices better than at the *Pietà*: as the choruses are wholly made up of female voices, they are never in more than three parts, often only in two; but these, when reinforced by the instruments, have such an effect, that the full complement to the chords is not missed, and the melody is much more sensible and marked by being less charged with harmony.[21]

The following week, the Mendicanti put on a concert specially for Burney:

> it was really curious to see as well to *hear* every part of this excellent concert, performed by female violins, hautbois, tenors, basses, harpsichords, french-horns, and even double basses. There was a prioress, a person in years, who presided: the first violin was very well played by Antonia Cubli, of Greek extraction; the harpsichord sometimes by

Francesca Rossi, *maestra di coro*, and sometimes by
others; these young persons frequently change instruments.[22]

Who else would have taught Maddalena? There were two other
teachers besides Bertoni who would have been important to her:
Antonio Barbieri (*c.* 1692–*c.* 1770), *maestro di maniera* who taught
singing, and Antonio Martinelli (*c.* 1710–83), *maestro di strumenti*.
Antonio Barbieri was appointed *maestro di maniera* in 1733, retiring
with a pension in 1767; he also taught at the Derelitti (or Ospedaletto).
He had had a successful singing career, including taking part in several
stage works by Antonio Vivaldi. There is a delightful caricature of him
by Anton Maria Zanetti in the library of the Fondazione Cini, on the
island of S. Giorgio, Venice. Antonio Martinelli must have lead a very
busy life. He also taught at the Derelitti and the Pietà, played the 'cello
in St Mark's orchestra, and composed instrumental music. Even for
Bertoni, the Mendicanti was not a full-time job, so he too had another
position, from 1752 that of first organist at St Mark's. In 1763 Barbieri
was paid 27 ducats, 12 grossi; Martinelli also 27 ducats, 12 grossi; but
Bertoni's salary was 87 ducats, 12 grossi. All were paid every three
months in arrears.[23] Maddalena would have been taught composition
by both Bertoni and Martinelli.

One of the many problems we have when writing about the *Ospedali*
is that so much of the music which was performed in their chapels and
concert rooms has been lost. An onlooker described the scene in
Venice on 16 May 1797, the last day of the Venetian Republic:

with my own eyes many years ago [I saw] books and
manuscripts being thrown from the windows of that place
[the Mendicanti] into waiting boats and transported away
by speculators who did not realize what they were taking.[24]

However, we do have the librettos of many of the oratorios which were
sung in their chapels, and often these give the names of the singers as
well as the librettist and composer. Unfortunately no names of
instrumentalists were given, so we have no record of Maddalena
playing, but in 1762 the Abbé Jérôme Richard was in Venice and wrote
the following description of a concert at the Mendicanti. The violinist
could well have been Maddalena:

[In the church] there are two well designed large balconies
or galleries. It is there that on Sundays and feast days the

> young girls sing a service which includes music or give
> oratorios which are a sort of spiritual concert. I have heard
> there the most perfect music, the most brilliantly executed
> and, according to me, the most beautiful women's voices
> of Italy . . . I saw there a twelve to thirteen-year-old—at
> most—young girl executing violin sonatas alone under
> general applause. One must have been confident in her
> talent to display it in public, on a solemn day before a
> sizeable audience. Only in Venice can one see these
> musical prodigies.[25]

In 1760, a new name appeared among the soloists, that of Lelia
Achiapati. Born in Brescia in 1745 she was an exact contemporary of
Maddalena, although she was only admitted into the Mendicanti on 1
January 1760 when she was fifteen. She must have been chosen
because of her exceptional ability as a singer and violinist. That year
she sang in a *Carmina Sacra* (devotionary songs) with music by
Bertoni. The following year she had the part of Nicodemus in the
oratorio *Mater Jesu, Juxta Crucem, Sacra Isagoge ad psalmum
Miserere Ad Usum Filiarum Nosocomii Sancti Lazari Mendicantium*,
again by Bertoni.[26] About 1768 she married the composer Pietro
Antonio Guglielmi, and we shall meet her again when both she and
Maddalena were performing in London.

Then, as now, Venice was notoriously unhealthy with heat and
humidity in the summer, fog, frost, and cold winds in the winter, so
periodically the *figlie* were allowed to go to the mainland to stay with a
family to recuperate. The first reference we have for Maddalena after
she entered the Mendicanti is for 4 June 1759 when a group of *figlie*,
accompanied by suitable chaperones—a sister, *zia d'educazione*, or
brother and sister-in-law were allowed to go "in villa" for a month "for
reasons of health". Among them were Maddalena Lombardini and
Chiara Variati accompanied by Signora Laura Martinelli. The Warden
was to be told that their usual bread, wine and other food was not to be
put out—the Mendicanti obviously did not like waste.[27] Maddalena
would surely have taken her violin with her, for the following year, 19
September 1760, the Governors were asked ". . . from Antonia Cubli
for permission to take "in villa" Lelia Achiapati in order to continue
her lessons while she is away".[28]

The lives of the *figlie* were probably not as dull as they might sound
to us. When important visitors came to Venice, the *Ospedali* took part

in entertaining them. Such a visit was that of Charles Eugene, Duke of Würtemberg, in January 1767:

> The Prince hired three palaces for himself and his suite. For merely fitting them up he paid the Jew Mandolini three hundred sequins a month. His suite consisted of seventy-five persons; some were gentlemen of birth, some officers, some musicians, and the rest servants. He was reported to have a couple of millions to spend. He brought a present of porcelain to his Excellency Giovanelli, worth sixty thousands florins. Marc Antonio Mocenigo, son of the Doge, as President of the pious foundation of the Mendicanti, gave a magnificent vocal and instrumental concert in the cloisters of the monastery, in honour of the Prince; it began at two o'clock of the night and ended at five, with sumptuous refreshments served during the performance.[29]

Regarding the times, the Venetians counted the hours from sunrise and sunset, so the concert probably began about 7:00 p.m. and ended about 10:00 p.m. An even more sumptuous affair took place in the Ca Rezzonico on 25 July 1769 for the visit of the Austrian Emperor Joseph II:

> What impressed Joseph II more than anything he had already seen was the sight awaiting him as he entered the grand ballroom . . . There, poised and waiting to begin were one hundred *figlie di coro* singers and instrumentalists from the four Venetian conservatoires. They were arranged in three balconies along one side of the hall. Violins, violoncellos, harps, and harpsichords were placed in the lowest balcony; winds, that is oboes, flutes, bassoons and traverse flutes, and brass, that is the trumpets and *corni di caccia* were in the top balcony with the percussion section. In the middle balcony Ferdinand Bertoni stood with the seven soloists and the chorus . . . Joseph II was so pleased with the performance that the very next day he contributed 220 Hungarian *regali* to be divided among the four hospitals.[30]

Edward Augustus, Duke of York and younger brother of George III, visited Venice in 1764. No elaborate descriptions of the musical entertainments provided for him have been found, but there is a receipt

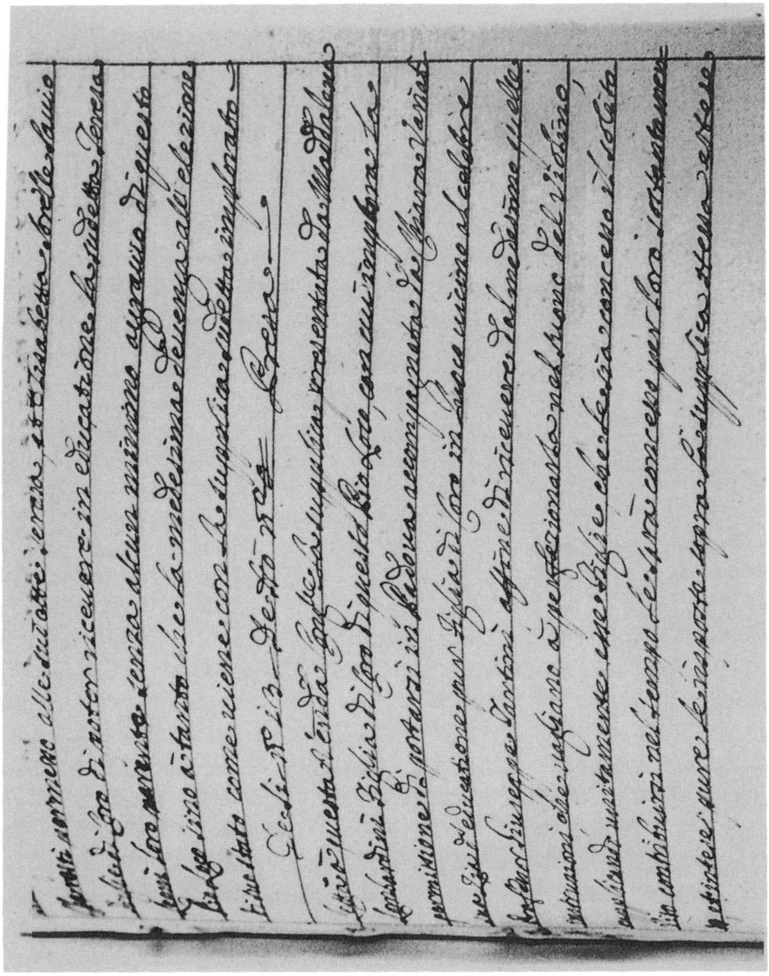

PERMISSION TO GO TO PADUA

dated 29 August 1764 and signed by Francesca Rossi, the *maestra di coro* of the Mendicanti, for payment of 60 lire for copying music to be performed in the two entertainments given by the *figlie* for the distinguished visitor.[31]

The *figlie* were paid for taking part in such entertainments. The money was put in the Mendicanti's bank, and when a *figlia* left, she was given her share. Individuals often left money for masses to be said for their souls after death, and the *figlie* were paid their share from those funds. For example, on 24 March 1763 Francesca Rossi, the *maestra di coro* received 100 lire 10 scudi to share among the *figliuoli di coro*.[32] Those leaving to get married each received a dowry of 137 ducats 12 grossi. Some of the *figlie*, not necessarily the *figlie di coro*, had substantial sums deposited in the bank and received interest every six months. For example, Catterina Bertola had the capital sum of 667 ducats in her account in 1763 and she received interest of 21 ducats 16 grossi for six months.[33] The bank seemed to have been thriving.

During the eighteenth century some unknown Venetians kept a diary which is now preserved in the Biblioteca Correr in Venice and known as the Codice Gradenigo. Here is part of the entry for 22 July 1766 showing how famous Maddalena was by then in Venice:

> The *figlie* of the *coro* of the *Ospedale de'Mendicanti* today as usual took part in the Festa of S. Maria Maddalena . . . Sig. Maddalena Lombardini, from Verona [*sic*] sang the Vespers, interspersed with some motets published and composed by the Doctor of Medicine Domenico Benedetti under the direction of Maestro Ferdinando Bertoni . . . [34]

We now come to the important event in Maddalena's life which has kept her name in the encyclopaedias and dictionaries of music—the letter to her from Giuseppe Tartini.

Notes

1. Venice, Archivio Patriarcale Raffaele, Battesimi, Reg. 1707–14, c.141. With many thanks to Gastone Vio for finding this document.
2. AP Raffaele, Matrimoni, Reg. 1734–68, 46.
3. AP Raffaele, Matrimoni, 47^r.
4. AP Raffaele, Battesimi, Reg. 1744–58, 25^r.

5. Venice, Istituzioni di Ricovero e di Educazione, Men. A.1 c.186. Quoted in *Arte*, 177.
6. Venice, Archivio di Stato, Ospedali e Luoghi Pii Diversi, Busta 872, 608.
7. IRE Men. B.1.c.146.
8. VAS, OLP, Busta 658, 17.3.1730.
9. Lord Ronald Sutherland Gower, tr., *Selections from the Letters of de Brosses* (London: Kegan Paul, 1897), 50–51.
10. IRE Men., A.5.N.6384.
11. IRE Men., B. 6.6560.
12. IRE Men., B.1.c.175 13.5.1676, quoted in *Arte*, 166 and 181.
13. Accademia dei Concordi, Rovigo, mss 96–6/19. Quoted in M.V. Constable, "The Venetian 'Figlie dei coro': their Environment and Achievement", *Music and Letters* (Vol. 63, 1982), 210–11.
14. IRE Men., B.1.c.175. Quoted in *Arte*, 166–67.
15. VAS, OLP, Busta 654, 27.8.1741.
16. VAS, OLP, Busta 655, 2.2.1744.
17. VAS, OLP, 21.9.1744.
18. IRE Men., A.6, n. 6312.
19. *History* IV, 514.
20. Hester Lynch Piozzi, *Observations and Reflections* (London: Strahan and Cadell, 1789), 145.
21. *Tour*, 141–42.
22. *Tour*, 183.
23. VAS, OLP, Busta 872.
24. C.G. Botta, *Storia d'Italia del 1789 al 1824* (Venice, 1826) quoted in N. Monferrato and G.F. Brusa, "Veneziani Maestri di Musica", *Archivio Veneto* (XI and XII, 1876), 258–76, 193–203.
25. L'Abbé Jérôme Richard, *Description Historique et Critique de L'Italie* (Dijon, 1766), 342.
26. Denis and Elsie Arnold, *The Oratorio in Venice* (London: The Royal Musical Association, 1986), 89.
27. IRE Men., B.7, n. 6827.
28. IRE Men., B.7, n. 6926.
29. Pompeo Molmenti tr., Horatio F. Brown, *Venice* (London: John Murray 1908), Part III, Vol. I, 112.
30. E.A. Cicogna, tr. J. Baldauf-Berdes, *Delle Iscrizioni Veneziane*, 7 vols. (Venice, 1825–53), IV, 550–51.
31. VAS, OLP, Busta 875, no. 675.
32. VAS, OLP, Busta 872, no. 543.
33. VAS, OLP, Busta 872, no. 503.

34. Venice, Museo Civico Correr, Codice Gradenigo 67, Tomo 16f 141v–142, 22 July 1766. I am indebted to Jonathan Glixon for drawing my attention to the entries in the Codice Gradenigo.

Chapter 3

TARTINI

Giuseppe Tartini (1692–1770) was probably the greatest influence on the life and career of Maddalena Lombardini Sirmen. She was among the last of his pupils and she must have seemed to him like the daughter he had never had. Tartini was born at Pirano in Istria. His early life seems rather mysterious, and what information we have comes from a manuscript written at the time of his death, probably by his friend, the cellist Antonio Vandini. He was meant to enter the church, and went as a student to Padua, but it is said he became a libertine, a fierce fencer, a duellist, quarrelsome, and the kidnapper of an innocent girl. In July 1710 he married Elizabetta Premazore, which put an end to any thought of an ecclesiastical career. She was the natural daughter of Cardinal Giorgio Cornaro, who was the Bishop of Padua, so in disgrace Tartini had to escape from the city to Assisi dressed as a pilgrim. In 1715 the authorities in Padua pardoned him, and in 1721 he was made *primo violino e capo di concerto* at the Basilica of S. Anthony. Apart from three years in Prague where the climate did not suit him, he spent the rest of his life in Padua. Here flourished his famous violin school.

Violin teachers at that time usually gave lessons in their pupils' homes; not so Tartini—his pupils had to come to him. Charles Burney said of him, "[he] had no other children than his scholars of whom his care was constantly paternal".[1] Students travelled from all over Europe:

27

France, Holland, Sweden, Germany—especially from Dresden—and even a certain Guglielmo Fegeri from as far away as Java (I am indebted to Pierluigi Petrobelli for this information). Tartini became famous as a brilliant violinist, a popular composer, and an internationally famous teacher. He taught members of the nobility, professional string players, and pupils from princely courts. In fact, the information he gleaned from his network of old students and friends throughout Europe was the equivalent of an eighteenth-century internet.

Burney tells the story of Tartini and his dream which became *The Devil's Trill*:

> He dreamed one night, in 1713, that he had made a compact with the Devil . . . he presented the Devil his violin . . . to his great astonishment, he heard him play a solo so singularly beautiful . . . it deprived him of the power of breathing. He awoke with the violence of his sensation, and instantly seized his fiddle, in hopes of expressing what he had just heard, but in vain: he, however, then composed a piece, which is perhaps the best of his works, he called it *The Devil's Sonata*.[2]

But Burney also gives a more sober account of Tartini's music in his *History*.

> Tartini, on a recent examination of his works, seems to my feelings and conceptions, to have had a larger portion of merit as a mere instrumental composer than any other author who flourished during the first fifty or sixty years of the present century. Though he made Corelli his model in the purity of his harmony, and simplicity of his modulation, he greatly surpassed that composer in the fertility and originality of his invention; not only in the subjects of his melodies, but in the truly cantabile manner of treating them. Many of his adagios want nothing but words to be excellent pathetic opera songs. His allegros are sometimes difficult; but the passages fairly belong to the instrument for which they were composed, and were suggested by his consummate knowledge of the finger-board, and powers of the bow. He certainly repeats his passages, and adheres to his original *motivo*, or *theme*, too much, for the favourite desultory style of the present times; but it must be allowed that by his delicate selection and arrangement of notes, his

passages are always good; play them quick or play them
slow, they never seem unmeaning or fortuitous.[3]

Tartini seems to have taught himself to play the violin. It was
common in families like the Vivaldis, for example, for the violin-
playing father to teach the son, but not in Tartini's case; his father was
not a professional violinist. During his lifetime Tartini wrote several
books about violin technique and music theory, which are interesting
but somewhat impersonal. He was also a prolific letter writer, and from
his letters we can see what a caring friend he was and how he was
always interested in other people. With his network of old pupils, he
was the centre of all the musical gossip of eighteenth-century Europe.
In one letter to Padre Martini at Bologna 9 June 1741, he asked him to
send six salami with garlic as a present to another friend, and in
another of 2 November 1736 he asked for some *rosolio* (special wine),
and a pair of ladies' stockings.[4] As recently as May 1994, a letter was
auctioned at Sotheby's, London. It was probably to Tartini's pupil,
Pietro Nardini, then in Vienna, asking him to look after two gentlemen
from Nuremberg who had been visiting him in Padua. The English
traveller Martin Folkes wrote in 1733:

> I was this evening at Sr Giustiniani's where was a concert
> of some of the most famous people particularly Sr Tartini
> of Padua said to be the finest violin in the world, I
> understand nothing but that I liked the instrument better
> than I have done, and they told me that he played and was
> the only one that could what they called a terza corda, that
> is, I think that he can stop three strings at once and to make
> one instrument do as it were three parts.[5]

And in 1769, another English traveller, T. Nugent, wrote:

> Naples had, for a long time, been the school and seminary
> of the best violins; yet they question their skill till they
> have been tried by the renowned Tartini, so that they flock
> to Padua to court his approbation. Tartini coolly hears
> them, and, after very attentive listening to what they pro-
> pose to execute, "That's fine", says he, or "that is very dif-
> ficult", that is "brilliantly executed, but", adds he, putting
> his fingers to his breast, "*it did not reach hither*".[6]

So Maddalena must have been a very accomplished violinist by
1760 to have approached Tartini for advice. Why he wrote this famous

letter to her, we do not know. It sounds as though the lessons had to be postponed. But strangely the letter is dated 5 March 1760 and, as far as we can tell, Maddalena only asked the Mendicanti Governors for permission to go to Padua to study with Tartini on 1 June 1760. Of course, Maddalena would not have received the letter straightaway; the *Priora* would have read it first, so perhaps there were lengthy discussions which have not been recorded about the advisability of the lessons, before the Governors were approached to give their permission. The other curious fact is how the letter came to be printed and published so widely. It could be that one of Tartini's pupils, realizing its importance, copied it before it was sent to Maddalena. In any case it is a splendid letter and gives us an insight into the teaching methods and thoughts of this exceptional man.

> Padua
> 5 March 1760

My very much esteemed Signora Maddalena,

> Finally, with God's will I have freed myself from that weighty business which has prevented me from keeping my word with you; although I wholeheartedly wanted to. Let me assure you that my failing was entirely due to lack of time, which in fact afflicted me. I have started this letter in the name of the Lord, and I continue by begging you to write to me if any explanations are unclear and ask for clarification on all the points that you do not understand.
>
> The first and most important exercise and practice is aimed at perfecting all bowing techniques; for you must have a good control of the bow whatever you play, whether as an orchestral player or to accompany singers . . . The bow should touch the string so lightly that the beginning of the note is like the sound of someone breathing rather than that of the string being hit. The success of this first contact depends on keeping the wrist very flexible and continuing the movement without hesitation, for when the first contact is light there is no danger that the bowing will be rough or crude.

And so it goes on. How to make crescendos and pianissimos, how useful it is to play Corelli's semi-quaver fugues (he was a great admirer of Corelli), how you use the left hand, how to play trills; and he ends:

For the moment, I would not recommend any other exercises: these are more than enough if your earnestness in practising them equals mine in recommending them to you. I hope you will let me know about your progress. For the time being, I send you my regards and beg you to pass them on to the Prioress (Fiorina Amorevoli), Signora Teresa (Bertoni's wife), and to Signora Chiara (Variati): all of whom are my friends.[7]

The Governors of the Mendicanti met on 1 June 1760:

consideration was given to a request from *figlia di coro* Maddalena Lombardini for permission to go to Padua with her *zia d'educazione* Chiara Variati . . . the plan is for them to live with *figlia* Lombardini's aunt and uncle in Padua in order that *figlia* Lombardini may study with the celebrated Professor Tartini. This would increase her ability as a violinist and so increase the value of her contribution to the *coro*. It is also requested that the above mentioned Chiara Variati should not remain in Padua so as to be a burden to Lombardini's relatives, but should return to Venice and continue in her regular role at the Conservatory once she has delivered Lombardini into her relatives' safe-keeping. Having considered the above mentioned document, the Deputy Governors grant their assent to the request. They also give their approval for the necessary charitable contribution for the above named Variati in view of the usefulness of *figlia* Lombardini, especially since this is an unusual cause with unusual circumstances pertaining to the service of the *coro* of this religious institution.

The Venerable Congregation graciously grants permission to the above-named Lombardini to go to Padua . . . in order to stay there for two months only . . . These permissions are granted in order that the results of Lombardini's study will reflect positively on the *coro* at the Mendicanti so that it will be able to profit from her studies with the celebrated teacher who has declared that he is willing to take her as a student, who, on her part has declared herself willing and eager to have the opportunity to receive Tartini's valuable instruction.[8]

One has the feeling that the idea of lessons from Tartini to Maddalena would be money well spent—a good investment, in fact. On the same day, other *figlie* were given permission to go "in villa"—to stay with a noble family on the mainland.[9]

There is no mention of any fee to be paid to Tartini, but there is a letter of Tartini to Padre Martini, dated 1739 regarding a possible pupil:

> The smallest honorarium I receive is two zecchini a month, and this is for violin only, while one pays three zecchini if one wants to learn counterpoint in addition. There are some students who pay me more but, as I have been saying, I am used to only two zecchini for violin lessons.[10]

There were two ways of travelling from Venice to Padua: by boat along the Brenta or by carriage. Burney went by carriage, and since he had to be careful about the money he spent during this travels, that was probably the most economical way. So it is highly likely that Maddalena and Chiara, too, travelled by *carozzina*. Burney describes it as "a kind of double open chaise. That part facing the horses has a cover to it—the other none . . . The fare to Fusina [from where you took a boat to Venice] is 18 lire".[11] A little earlier in his account Burney says that "there are 22 lire in a zecchin which is a little more than 9s English".[12] Burney says about Padua:

> the entrance into this town is very disagreeable, the streets narrow, dark, and diabolically paved, with great rumbling stones of different sizes. At a distance, however, the public buildings afford a fine prospect: I counted near 30 tho' seen from a flat. It is remarkable for its porticos almost thro' the town, which are low and render the ground floors very dark, but yet they are not only convenient in wet weather but I found by experience their use in *hot* weather.[13]

The lessons must have been a great success. We can only imagine how stimulating it must have been for Maddalena to have a new teacher, and such a famous one. She would also take advantage of Tartini's fame as a composer to have lessons in composition. One imagines that her playing must have improved considerably, since the following year there was no opposition from the Governors when she asked permission to go to Padua again for more lessons with Tartini.[14] There are no records of her having lessons in 1762 and 1763 but they could very well have been lost. At the Governors meeting on 29 August 1764:

> There was read to the venerable congregation the supplication presented by Maddalena Lombardini, *figlia di coro* of this religious institution by which she begs permission to go to Padua in the company of Chiara Variati, her *zia d'educazione* and fellow member of the *coro*, in order to study with the famous Professor Giuseppe Tartini to profit from his instruction in order to perfect her violin playing skills. The two *figlie* also ask for an allowance to cover their living expenses . . .
>
> In consideration of the highly important objective underlying this proposal which is to add to the skills gained through previous study *figlia* Lombardini has had with Tartini with which she was able to enhance her usefulness to our musical ensembles and add to their high reputation, the Governors decree that *figlie* Lombardini and Variati be permitted to go to Padua and to receive the usual allowance granted by this religious institution, as required by this highly unusual situation and in accordance with the precedent set in the case of *figlia* Lombardini on 1 June 1760.

But it took three ballots for the Governors to agree that permission should be given, and then only after they had decided not to finance the trip.[15] So who paid her expenses? We do not know, but it sounds as though there might have been a nobleman who took an interest in her and who financed the visit. Among the Governors at that time were members of such famous Venetian families as Marcello, Dolfin, Corner, and Mocenigo, any of whom might have helped. The Codice Gradenigo in the entry for 31 January 1765 (MV) states:

> Maddalena Lombardini, among the *figlie* placed in the *Ospedale de'Mendicanti* had taken great advantage of the education offered there, and in addition at the age of twenty years, she is known as the best violin player of all the violinists in the *coro*, and was the pupil of the famous Maestro Giuseppe Tartini of Pirano in Istria.[16]

Two years later at a meeting of the Governors on 1 June 1766 we read:

> gracious permission be granted to the undersigned to go to the various villas accompanied by their chaperones whose

names appear below. The visits will be for no longer than one month. This permission is valid for one time only and in the current season. The *Priora* should deliver these *figlie* to the appropriate persons on the day of their departure. Notice of their absence should be given to the domestic staff so that their portions of food and wine should not be wasted. The *Priora* is also to give notice of the girls' return in time for them to prepare for the day of S. Maria Maddalena. Those *figlie* given permission to leave are:

> Maddalena Lombardini, accompanied by Chiara Variati and by the noblewoman Cecilia Valmarana, on the advice of our doctor.[17]

Notes

1. *Tour*, 123.
2. *Tour*, 122–123.
3. *History* III, 566.
4. L. Busi, *Il Padre G.B. Martini* (Bologna: Zanichelli, 1891).
5. Oxford Bodleian Library mss. Eng. Misc. c444, 35–36.
6. *New Observations on Italy* (London, 1769), II, 393.
7. A complete translation of the letter and its publishing history are included in appendixes B and C.
8. IRE Men., A.7, n. 6908.
9. IRE Men., A.7, n. 6908.
10. F. Parisini, *Carteggio Inedito del P. Giambattista Martini* (Bologna, 1888).
11. *Poole*, 72.
12. *Poole*, 69.
13. *Poole*, 67.
14. IRE Men., B.7, n. 6827 and n. 6985.
15. IRE Men. B.7, n. 7139.
16. Codice Gradenigo 67, Tomo 15, f 118v–119.
17. IRE Men., B.7, n. 7253.

Chapter 4

MARRIAGE

In 1766 Maddalena was twenty years old. What future could she expect? She had been made a teacher, *maestra*, by this time and could, if she wanted, remain in the Mendicanti for the rest of her life. We have the example of Margherita Buonafede who was admitted to the *coro* in 1733, not as an orphan, but, like Maddalena, as a musician:

> her voice has all those qualities deemed desirable, such as a soprano range equally reliable and clean at both the highest and lowest ranges, a natural ability to trill, and perfect pitch. There is every reason to expect that she will develop into an excellent singer, one who will make an extra-ordinarily valuable contribution to the *coro*.[1]

And the Governors were right. Galuppi wrote a solo motet, a *Salve Regina* for Margherita Buonafede in 1746, and she was still singing in 1765 for the festival of S. Maria Maddalena.[2] Maddalena must have known her well. Alternatively a *figlia* could become a nun, or get married. Maddalena chose to get married.

What do we know about her husband, Lodovico Sirmen?[3] The name Sirmen/Syrmen/Cirmen does not sound Italian, but Gaetano Ravaldini suggests that soldiers from the Swiss Guards were in Ravenna from about 1517; and other non-Italian sounding names are to be found there such as Tanner, Zimmermann, Sutter, and Jenuscki, etc.

We have Lodovico's certificate of baptism:

Ravenna 13 November 1738

> On this day Lodovico Maria Gaspar, son of Giovanni
> Mateo, son of Signor Melchior Syrmen and his legal wife
> Alessandra, daughter of the late Hicronymus Pillastrini,
> was born 11pm on November 12, 1738, and baptised today
> by Father Damiani Bastatiani of S. Euphemia's church.
> The godparents were Signor Laurentius Serra, son of
> Antonio, and Maria Contarini, daughter of the late
> Domenico. Assisting was I, the undersigned Prospero
> Guardi of S. Giovanni in Fonte, the ecclesiastical official
> for baptisms.[4]

Lodovico was the fifth of ten children and seems to have come from
a comfortable background. His mother wrote poetry and her work can
be found in contemporary anthologies. In Ravenna she presided over a
salon for local intellectuals including the Rector of the College of
Nobles, Fillipo Bellardi, and the local medical doctor, Count Ruggero
Calbi.[5] Lodovico may have studied the violin under Paolo Alberghi
(1716–85)—another pupil of Tartini who came to work in Ravenna
from Faenza and was there 1758–61. In 1765 Lodovico was working in
Mantua and during the following year he gave a concert in Bergamo.
He undoubtedly impressed his sponsors since they encouraged him to
apply for the post of Violin Teacher and First Violinist in the Basilica
of S. Maria Maggiore. Something very peculiar was happening in
Bergamo. Lodovico must have had some extremely influential friends
among the governing body since at the first ballot one Giovanni
Battista Rovelli of Bergamo was appointed to the post by nine votes to
six whilst Lodovico only got six in favour and nine against. A week
later:

> Today's meeting of the executive committee of the
> religious institution resulted in the setting aside of the
> election results taken on 21 January to determine according
> to the by-laws, the election of a new First Violinist . . .
> First, members celebrated Mass of the Holy Spirit this
> morning and heard a solemn singing of the liturgy in the
> church of S. Maria Maggiore. There was a reading of
> Chapter III, Part 1 by the President who asked for prudent
> reflection on the part of those present with regard to the
> results of the previous election so that no one would be

forced to intervene in the forthcoming vote. Lodovico Cirmen has amply demonstrated his skill and value to his profession by coming here to perform from Mantua as soloist in his own concertos. Having done so he now seeks the post of First Violinist in the Cappella Maggiore. His aspiration has met with universal support and applause from the citizens of Bergamo who have made known their enthusiasm for his election to representatives of this body. The matter of whether a larger or smaller number of musicians in the Cappella are natives of Bergamo should not be the main consideration of his appointment even though the by-laws do specify that one of our own citizens should have the post of First Violinist.

Whatever has been decided by the election of G. B. Rovelli to the post of First Violinist may be adapted by appointing Lodovico Cirman as another member of the first violin section and giving him the same salary, privileges, and other prerogatives as those traditional for the First Violinist. In this way, the foreigner, Lodovico Cirmen could have the position along with the title of First Violinist and Director of the Orchestra without offending anybody. His salary will be the same as Rovelli's; in such cases where difference in treatment may arise, it will be the responsibility of the *Signori Deputati* of the church to find ways to treat the two musicians as equals without offending the interests of either of them.[6]

Lodovico must have had considerable charm! But we must feel sorry for the *Signori Deputati*. It seems worthwhile quoting most of these documents to show how appointments could be made in the eighteenth century—perhaps at times not too different from the twentieth . . . However, the account does show that Lodovico was by no means a nobody when he met Maddalena.

A document exists in the *Curia Patriarcale di Venezia* showing that Maddalena and an unnamed suitor had petitioned to be married, but that no action could be taken because she was under twenty-one years old.[7] According to the document permission was refused for the marriage, since Maddalena's father had not appeared to give his consent. In fact, Piero Lombardini had died sometime earlier, probably around 1762, so there is a feeling that permission was being deliberately withheld by the Mendicanti. Why, after all, should they lose Maddalena when they had spent so much money on her education?

Also, she was supposed to stay at the Mendicanti for ten years after her training had finished. And we do not know whether she had as yet taught two other *figlie* to take her place as she had promised when she had been admitted to the *coro* in 1753.

Now her beloved Tartini took matters into his own hands. One of his old students, Giovanni Gottlieb Naumann, was Court Composer of Sacred Music to the Dowager Electress Marie-Antoinette (referred to as H.R.H.) at Dresden, and on 3 October 1766 Tartini wrote to him to try to get Maddalena a post there:

> Whenever H.R.H. pleases to wish for the young violinist at the Mendicanti to enter her service, the simplest way is to ensure her marriage with a certain Giuseppe Scoti of Cremona, a tenor singer with a good voice, ready to marry her. By statute, the Holy House of the Mendicanti never allows the removal of girls educated there, except to become nuns or get married. In the latter case, strict enquiry is made, whether the circumstances of the man are such as to enable him to maintain his wife respectably; and if she be a singer, the husband must give security that she shall never be made to appear for hire at a theatre. Here there is no difficulty, because this girl is a player and not a singer. The difficulty is with the man who can give no security as to his circumstance, except his art itself of singing; and this is not enough to satisfy the law of the Holy House . . . It would be amply sufficient if he could be established in the service of some court, and then the Holy House would shut its eyes and give him the girl to wife . . . this girl, one of admirable and even saintly conduct, and of that singular ability on the violin . . . since among all the many scraping scholars that I have had . . . for practised violin playing which goes to the heart, this girl only is at this present moment absolutely without equal.

Tartini then goes on to propose a positively Machiavellian plot to get Maddalena and Scoti into the service of the Dresden court. He ends the letter quite pathetically:

> The poor child, so much slandered and envied in the Holy House, as you yourself have seen with your own eyes, has no other wish but to escape out of it, in order not to die of madness, or something worse; and indeed she will certainly seize the first opportunity which offers for doing so. It is

true, that both she and I are agreed in desiring to secure her engagement by H.R.H., even at an allowance which should be less by one-half than she could obtain at any other court; but, where it is a question of saving life, one clings even to thorns, as the proverb goes. I confess to you moreover that, if the clemency of our Sovereign Mistress consents to the plan proposed so that this pupil of mine may have the good luck to be received into Her service, this will be the greatest consolation of my old age.[8]

So, if Tartini is to be believed, Maddalena was desperate to leave the Mendicanti and it was not unusual for *figlie* to leave to get married. They received a dowry of 137 ducats, 12 grossi and their share of the money they had received from outside engagements with the *coro* and from trusts.

Nearly a year later at a meeting of the Governors on 24 August 1767 we learn:

The Congregation has listened to the report of the *maestro e maestra di coro* and they will not allow Maddalena Lombardini, a violinist of the *coro* to marry Lodovico Sirmen, son of Giovanni Matteo of Ravenna: 6 for, 8 against.[9]

But three and a half weeks later, they relented and permission was given:

There was read to this Venerable Congregation the request submitted by Lodovico Sirmen together with enclosed documents related to his desire to marry Maddalena Lombardini, a *figlia di coro*, and to receive the usual dowry coming from benefactor's bequests. He begs the Venerable Congregation to consent to graciously grant him this wish. He also presents a true affadavit for his parents' consent to his marriage. The contents of all the documents submitted by Sirmen were discussed by the worthy Governors serving on the Committee over the *figlie* concerning the habits, status, and professional position of Lodovico Sirmen, as well as the service provided to this institution's music activities by the violinist Lombardini. Statements in support of Sirmen's request have been submitted, as is required.

16 September 1767 the Governors recommend that Lodovico Sirmen's request be granted. It will be the duty of the Committee to carry out the process once consent has been assured from *La Lombardina* to whom belongs the

137 ducats, 12 grossi dowry which will be disbursed after
the marriage by our Treasurer Count Algarotti. A receipt is
to be signed to protect this religious institution.[10]

Here are the documents:

The following statements concerning the eligibility of
Maddalena Lombardini, daughter of the late Piero
Lombardini, Venetian, aged 22, born into the faith in the
Church of S. Raffaelo Arcangelo and now a member of S.
Maria Formosa parish, is the sworn testimony of the
witness:

Thomas Rovantini, son of the late Charles, has lived
in Venice, within the S. Cassiano district. He is 48
years of age. The witness responded to the examiner's
request to appear before him in support of an
application by Maddalena Lombardini to marry
willingly. Asked if he knows Signora Maddalena,
and, if so, how well and for how long, he answers that
he has known Signora Maddalena for many years in
the Mendicanti hospital where he has met her on
frequent occasions and has also been her French
teacher. Asked if Signora Maddalena has ever been
married, answers no. Asked the reason as far as he
knows, for the marriage, he replies, I know the
reasons have to do with her money deposited [in the
Mendicanti's bank], and the matter of her rightful
dowry, I certainly should know it.

(signed) Thomas Rovantini

Francesco Gottardi . . . has known Signora Maddalena as
maestra of the *figlie di coro* at the Mendicanti where she
has worked in this capacity for about six years . . . Asked
for the reasons for the forthcoming marriage, he says it is
for Maddalena's dowry which, because it is unusually
large, she fears might be spent and thus denied her. He
swears that what he says is true and spoken in good faith.

(signed) Francesco Gottardi.[11]

On 20 September, the couple exchanged vows in the church of S.
Maria Formosa:

17 September 1767

All three readings of the banns being dispensed with by the
Most Reverend Father Bartolomeo Trevisan, Vicar General, according to regulations on file, a true and legitimate
marriage with the exchange of vows took place before
those present between Signora Maddalena Laura, daughter
of the late Pietro Lombardini, a Venetian, who is of this
parish, and Lodovico, son of Signor Giovanni Sirmen of
Ravenna. This Sirmen serves in the retinue of the
nobleman Domenico Cavagnis, son of the late Antonio
Cavagnis, of this parish. Their marriage was officiated over
by the Reverend Signor Don Giacomo Merossi, Titular
Deacon of the church and licensed parish priest. The
couple consented and then exchanged vows in the presence
of the Nobleman Domenico Cavagnis and Father Domenico Bellotto, Titular Priest and under-sacristan of the
church. On September 20, 1767, a nuptial Mass was celebrated in the Oratory of the Women's Cloister in the
Ospedale dei Mendicanti. The Mass was celebrated by
Reverend Father Don Girolamo Scotti, Somaschian priest
and Hospital Rector, with the traditional bestowal of the
nuptial blessing in the presence of the above-named
witnesses.[12]

And the wedding was so important that it was reported in the Codice
Gradenigo:

The Wedding is announced from the *Congregazione del
Pio Ospitale de'Mendicanti* of the virtuoso Maddalena
Lombardini from the *figliole del Coro*, the most eminent
and best performer on the violin.[13]

Why did the Governors of the Mendicanti change their minds so
quickly? Was she pregnant? There was certainly a daughter, Alessandra, named after her paternal grandmother, born in the early years of
their marriage, but no birth certificate has so far been found. Was
Maddalena having a nervous crisis as Tartini's letter seems to hint, or,
had she accumulated so much money in the Mendicanti's bank that
there was not enough cash available to pay her when she left? If this
was true, perhaps one of the Mendicanti's wealthy governors had
stepped in with money to help the bank. This is, of course, all pure
speculation.

One wonders how she and her husband met. Lodovico Sirmen, six months after his appointment in Bergamo in 1766, was given leave of absence for five weeks beginning in June. This leave happened to coincide with the time that Maddalena was given permission to go "in villa" for a month with the "noblewoman Cecilia Valmarana". We do not know which Villa Valmarana they went to, but there is the possibility that Maddalena and Lodovico met there. Or they could have met in Venice. As we have seen, the choirs and orchestras of the *ospedali* were available for concerts outside their own buildings, and Maddalena and Lodovico could have met at one of the "academies" or concerts held in a private palace. After all, according to the wedding documents, Lodovico seems to have been employed by Domenico Cavagnis in Venice. Or, were they introduced by Tartini? As far as we know, Lodovico was never his pupil but some of Lodovico's music is to be found in Padua, and, of course, Tartini had friends everywhere. I think this is the most likely explanation.

Maddalena and Lodovico's descendants in Ravenna have two miniature pastel portraits, one each of Maddalena and Lodovico, but undated, so we do not know how old they were when they were made. Lodovico looks rather dashing with grey hair swept back into a tidy roll, an unbuttoned pink jacket and a shirt with frilly lace showing, some music in his hand, and a smile on his face. Maddalena appears rather severe with grey hair—I suppose they both could have had powdered hair—piled on top of her head and then neatly formed into rolls either side of her face. Over this, she wears a pretty bonnet with salmon pink trimming which seems to be fastened with some sort of jewel, and a jacket of the same colour with a fur collar—altogether a very elegant lady.

And so she left the Mendicanti, taking copies of her compositions with her. She had cause to be very grateful indeed to the Governors and all the *maestri* who had taught her so well. As a composer she was extremely fortunate to have lived in a community where she had at her disposal an orchestra of professional standards happy to perform her violin concertos with herself as soloist. Her quartets, duets, and trios are a pleasure to play nowadays, so we can imagine her fellow musicians enjoying music specially written for them. She was probably very much missed by the community but we can imagine her delight in the freedom which she had gained.

Notes

1. IRE Men., A.6, n. 5099, 3.5.1733.
2. Denis Arnold, "A *Salve* for Signora Buonafede," *Journal of the Royal Musical Association*, 113, part 2 (1988), 168–71.
3. Most of the information about Lodovico is to be found in three sources: the manuscripts of I. Gamba Ghiselli, *De fatti di Ravenna* . . . 15 vols., in the *Archivio Storico Communale di Ravenna*, mss. RAasc Gamba n. 65; Pompeo Raisi, *Giornale* . . . mss. RAc Mob. 3. 2. M/2; and P. Uccellini's *Dizionario Storico di Ravenna* (Ravenna: Tipografia del Seminario Arcivescovale, 1855). These sources are quoted in *Fabbri*. Jane Berdes was also given helpful information by Gaetano Ravaldini of Ravenna.
4. Ravenna Battezzati S. Barbara XVII. Indice S. c.107r.
5. *Ghiselli* VI, cc.18^v–19^r.
6. Bergamo Misericordia Archive (M.I.A.) LXIII, Terminazione N.1296 cc.251^v–252^r.
7. ACP, 1767, II, Indice 342.
8. Julian Marshall, "Tartini and Maddalena Syrmen," *The Queen, the Lady's Newspaper* (26 March 1892). Readers may be interested to know that this magazine was the precursor of *Harper's Bazaar*.
9. IRE Men., B, n. 7312.
10. IRE Men., B, n. 7320.
11. IRE Men., B, n. 7320.
12. AP Formosa, Reg. 1715–78, IX c. 4224.
13. 67, Tomo 19, f18, 16.9.1767.

Chapter 5

HONEYMOON TRAVELS

The first information we have of Maddalena and Lodovico after their marriage is from the archives at Faenza.[1] In 1767 a local priest, Monsignor Giovanni Carlo Boschi of Faenza, was elected to be Cardinal of *S. Lorenzo in Lucina e Penitenziere Maggiore*, and the event was celebrated for nearly three months, obviously a case of "local boy makes good". On 31 August Cardinal Boschi arrived in Faenza and remained there until 20 October. His arrival was celebrated with fireworks, *conversazioni nobili*, music, and a greasy pole-climbing contest with a prize of a purse filled with gold pieces and a huge horn-of-plenty filled with *commestibili squisiti e liquori inesauribili*.

On 11 October there was a great *festa* in the Piazza, given by Faentine merchants who provided poultry, birds, beef and roasted pork, cheese, four barrels of wine, and four thousand loaves of bread. In the evening there was an *accademia*, or concert, in Cardinal Boschi's Palazzo, where a cantata of Alberghi was performed with two soloists, the soprano Loranzo Tonarelli and contralto Sabastiani Emiliani, Virtuoso to the Elector of Bavaria. Then, Maddalena Sirman, "*educata nel Conservatorio di Ve[nezia] fece un concerto di violino*".[2] Who wrote the concerto? Was it by Maddalena herself, Lodovico, or Alberghi? Maddalena must have been reasonably well known to have been invited to play at such an important event. The concert was only three and a half weeks after their wedding. Did Lodovico take her home to meet his family in Ravenna, or was the whole thing engineered by Tartini?

We next hear of the Sirmens in Turin. In 1768 they set out on a European concert tour accompanied by Don Giuseppe Terzi. As Maddalena said in her will, dated 9 June 1798, "Since Don G. Terzi has lived with me from the time of my marriage, I wish that he may never be obliged by any person to be held to account for anything that may have belonged to me". He could have been one of the *mansionari* to the Mendicanti—one of the priests used by the *ospedali* to celebrate the many memorial Masses paid by legacies, but we have no documentary evidence for this. Maddalena must have been very fond of him judging by the references to him in her wills. Perhaps Terzi and Maddalena had struck up a firm friendship during her many years at the Mendicanti, and after the wedding he could very well have been asked to become her *cavaliere servente* or *cicisbeo*. To try to explain the term, here is part of a letter by Anna, Lady Miller who toured Italy in 1770–71:

> [Venice] the custom of *Cavalieri Serventi* prevails universally here: this usage would appear in a proper light, and take off a great part of the odium thrown upon the Italians, if the *Cavalieri Serventi* were called husbands, for the real husband, or beloved friend of a Venetian lady (often for life), is the *cicisbeo*. The husband married in church is the choice of her friends, not by any means of the lady. It is from such absurd tyranny of the relations and friends of young girls, not suffering them to chuse for themselves, that this chusing of *Cicisbeos* or *Cavalieri Serventis* has taken its rise, and will never be relinquished in Italy, whilst the same incongruous combinations subsist: this surely lessens the criminality, at least in some degree.[3]

So off they went, the three of them, to Turin. Maddalena was twenty-three, Lodovico, thirty, and Terzi, thirty-two, and since they must have been comfortably off, they would have had their servants too. It must have been a jolly party.

Turin at this time was an important musical centre; the capital city of Piedmont, which was part of the Kingdom of Sardinia. There were two theatres: the opera house—the Teatro Reggio—and a smaller Teatro Carignano. The main route to and from Paris into Italy passed through the city, so that musicians who had been performing in Paris at the

Concert Spirituel frequently played in Turin during their travels. The King, Carlo Emanuele III, was patron of the woodwind-playing Besozzi family, the oboe- and bassoon-playing brothers Alessandro (1702–93) and Paolo Girolamo (1704–78) spent much of their lives in Turin. Their nephew Gaetano (1727–98) played in Paris at the same *Concert Spirituel* as the Sirmens in 1768, and another member of the family, Carlo, worked at Dresden from 1755–92. Perhaps he was helpful in getting Maddalena appointed a singer there in 1779. The violinist and composer Gaetano Pugnani (1731–98) also spent much of his life in Turin, though he was probably in Paris when the Sirmens paid their visit. Samuel Sharp, a distinguished surgeon, was in Turin on 19 May 1766, and he wrote:

> The good old king in his latter days, gives himself up
> entirely to devotion . . . and the chief splendour of the city
> is to be found in the King's chapel. He has a choice
> Orchestra, at the head of which are *Pugnani* and the two
> *Biscoucis*. He seldom prays to God, but as *Nebuchadnezzar*
> prayed to his God, with the sound of the sachbut, the
> psalter, and all kinds of musical instruments.[4]

Samuel Johnson said of Sharp's letters that there was a "great deal of matter in them".

Charles Burney, for once, was not too critical when he passed through Turin on his way to Milan in 1770:

Thursday, 12 July 1770

> The language here is half French and half Italian, but both
> corrupted. This cannot be applied to the music which is
> pure Italian, and Turin has produced a Giardini [Maddalena
> was to meet Felice Giardini in London]; there are likewise
> at present in this city the famous *Dilettante*, Count Bene-
> vento, a great performer on the violin, and a good compos-
> er; the two Besozzis, and Pugnani; all, except the Count, in
> the service of the King of Sardinia. Their salary is not
> much above eighty guineas a year each, for attending the
> chapel royal; but then the service is made very easy for
> them, as they only perform solos there, and those just when
> they please. The *Maestro di Capella* is Don Quirico Gas-
> parini. In the chapel there is commonly a symphony played
> every morning, between eleven and twelve o'clock by the
> king's band which is divided into three orchestras, and

played in three different galleries; and though far separated from each other, the performers know their business so well that there is no want of a person to beat time, as in the opera and *Concert Spirituel* at Paris . . . On festivals Signor Pugnani plays a solo, or the Besozzis a duet, and sometimes motets are performed with voices. The organ is in the gallery which faces the king, and in this stands the principal first violin.[5]

Although Burney also mentioned the fact that:

The grand place (with the king's palace, which entirely fills one side, and the palace of *Madame* in the middle, both of white stone) built it is said from the designs of Vignola, are very fine and striking, but amidst all this grandeur I am so devoured by flies, fleas, and bugs that I cannot get a wink of sleep.[6]

but on Saturday, 14 July:

Signor Pugnani played a concerto this morning at the king's chapel . . . I need say nothing of the performance of Signor Pugnani, his talents are too well known in England to require it. I shall only observe, that he did not appear to exert himself: and it is not to be wondered at as neither His Sardinian Majesty, nor any one of the numerous royal family seem at present to pay much attention to music.[7]

The Sirmens' patron was probably Count Benvenuto di S. Raffaele. He was Minister of Education for Savoy and had been a pupil of Tartini. He composed sonatas, corresponded with Tartini over the years, and wrote a treatise on the art and theory of violin playing in the form of *Lettere due sopra l'arte del suono, del Sig. Conte Benvenuto di S. Rafaele, torinese. In Vicenza, 1778, per Antonio Veronese.*[8] It was to him that the Sirmen *Six String Quartets* were dedicated when they were published a little later in Paris. Bertoni, Maddalena's teacher at the Mendicanti, also had connections with Turin. His new opera, *Tancredi* had been highly successful during the previous year's carnival, so presumably the Sirmens were hardly an unknown couple of performers when they arrived, and, as far as we can tell, Maddalena was the first woman violinist to play there in public. The Sirmens, probably, as was the custom, first performed privately for the royal family and other members of the nobility before their first public concert. Again, Samuel Sharp wrote:

> There are two theatres at *Turin*; the one for the serious opera, almost as large and magnificent as that at *Naples*; the second, a smaller, for the three other kinds of Spectacles, namely, the *Comedie Françoise*, the *Comedie Italienne*, and the *Opera Comique*. These four exhibitions succeeded each other in the four different seasons of the year; but the King and Family never frequent any but the Grand Opera . . . There is a society of forty Gentlemen, answerable for every expense whatsoever, *viz.* the salaries of the actors and the orchestra, the purchase of the scenery, the dresses, etc., etc. so that the performers are sure of their pay, though the opera should not succeed. It is not so with regard to the *Italian* and *French* comedians, those two companies taking the chance of good and bad houses.[9]

So Lodovico had to write to the *Cavalieri* who managed the Teatro Carignano, the smaller of the two theatres.

> May 31, in the Year of Our Lord, 1768. Members present are Counts Porporato, and d'Aglie, Marquis Beggiamo, and Cavalier di Salmor—, Lodovico Sirmen from Ravenna, together with his wife, both violin virtuosi, wish to give a public concert next Friday, 3 June, in the Teatro Carignano. They ask leave to perform in the manner followed by other visiting artists, that is, they will deduct from their gross receipts expenses for door-keepers, complimentary tickets for the military, lighting, etc., and musicians' salaries. A four-fifths share of the profits will go to the virtuoso Sirmen and his wife, the other fifth to the *Società de'Signori Cavalieri*. Permission for the above was granted on the condition that Lodovico Sirmen must first obtain written permission for the concert from *Monsignore Arci-vescovo*.[10]

The significant part of this document is the mention of "musicians' salaries". Maddalena and Lodovico were therefore presumably going to play violin concertos which needed an orchestra. Quirino Gasparini (1720–78) was a composer of operas as well as being *Maestro di Cappella*. The opera orchestra consisted of fifty-three instrumentalists: thirty-eight string players, two bassoons, four oboes, four "corni da caccia", two trumpets, two keyboards, and one percussionist, so presumably there was no difficulty for the Sirmens to form an orchestra. In the season 1766–67, poor Gasparini only earned L.700 for his opera *Mitridate re di Ponto* while Bertoni, Maddalena's old teacher at the Mendicanti, received L.1230 for *Tancredi*. He must have been a very popular composer, no wonder Maddalena had profited from her lessons with him.[11] Incidentally, Mozart used the same libretto for his opera, *Mitridate*, performed in Milan in 1770.

We do not know how many times the couple performed in Turin, but on 22 June Quirino Gasparini wrote to his friend Padre Martini at Bologna:

> To give you some news of this area: the distinguished Signora Maddalena Lombardini who studied the violin with Signor Giuseppe Tartini, has been here for a few days. She is from the Conservatorio of the Mendicanti in Venice and is married to a certain Lodovico Sirmen who is first violinist at the Capella at Bergamo. She won the admiration of all Turin with her violin playing. She left today with her husband for France. She was very pleased to have received gifts and other valuables to the value of 400 zecchini. Last Saturday I wrote to old Tartini at Padua telling him of this; it will satisfy him and make him happy, especially since the violinist performs his sonatas with such perfection that she proves herself to be his true and worthy descendant.[12]

Their next stop was Paris. In these days of easy travel we read with admiration and amazement of the difficulties of crossing the Alps. Samuel Sharp's description of the Mount Cenis pass is graphic:

> Mount *Cenis* . . . Both going and returning, when you arrive at the foot of the hill, your coach, or chaise, is taken to pieces and carried on mules to the other side, and you yourself are transported by two men, on a common straw elbow chair, without any feet to it, fixed upon two poles, like a sedan chair, with, however, a swinging foot-board to prop up your feet; but, though it be the work of two men only to carry you, six, and sometimes eight attend, in order to relieve one another. The whole way that you ride in this manner being fourteen or fifteen miles, when the person carried is corpulent, it is necessary to employ ten porters.[13]

According to Thomas Martyn's *The Gentleman's Guide to his Tour through Italy*, it took thirteen hours forty minutes to travel the fifty-two miles from Mont Cenis to Turin and from there, about another 350 miles or so to Paris.[14]

One wonders how many days it took them to reach Paris. The most important series of concerts in Paris at that time were the *Concert Spirituel*, founded in 1725 by Anne-Danican Philidor (1681–1728) and held in the *Salle des Suisses* at the Tuileries. In 1768 the director of the concerts was Antoine Dauvergne (1713–97), whose programmes were typical of the period—a mixture of symphonies, suites, concertos and songs. Women composer/violinists were not unknown in Paris. Elizabeth de Haulteterre played Leclair's sonatas at the *Concert Spirituel* in 1737 "with all imaginable intelligence, vivacity and precision".[15] She was also a composer, writing concertos and sonatas for the violin, but unfortunately none of her compositions have survived. On 8 September 1750, "*Mme Tasca, Vénitienne, de la musique de l'Empereur, joua seulement le 8 Sept . . . des oeuvres de sa composition*". A Venetian, like Maddalena, she played a concerto written by herself "in the style of Vivaldi"—perhaps she had been one of his pupils.[16]

Probably a good deal of excitement was generated by the thought of a beautiful young woman playing the violin in a public concert. The publicity-conscious management of the *Concert Spirituel* made Maddalena promise not to perform in public in Paris before her first concert for them on 15 August 1768. Here is the programme:

> Symphony
>
> Diligam te—Gilles
>
> Concerto for oboe played by (Gaetano) Besozzi
>
> *Coeli enarrant* a little motet for solo voice sung by the abbé Durais of St-Germain l'Auxerrois
>
> Concerto for 2 violins played by Mme Sirmen and the composer
>
> Italian airs with latin words sung by Mlle Fel, with an oboe accompaniment by Besozzi
>
> *Exultate justi by* Dugué (Mme Larrivée)
>
> Gélin and Muguet sang during the concert.[17]

Unfortunately, the music for the double concerto has been lost.

An anonymously written review of this concert appeared on Monday, 22 August, in Louis Petit de Bachaumont's *Mémoires secrets, pour servir à l'histoire de la république des lettres en France.*[18]

> The *Concert Spirituel* was exceptionally brilliant today; the audience was attracted by the spectacle of a woman playing the violin. Mme Sireman, a young and pretty Venetian, performed a double concerto with her husband which they had composed. The management had insisted prior to the performance that she was not to perform anywhere else in order to intensify curiosity. She was applauded loudly. One found truth, purity, and gentleness in her playing. Especially in the Adagio, she played with a sensitivity which is characteristic of her sex. Certainly she has taken the violin so far in the direction of perfection that one is hard put to name any of the great masters who could play better or even as well as she does.

A second review appeared in *L'Avant Coureur* on 22 August, p. 540:

> M. and Mme Siremen played a double violin concerto of their own composition. Mme Siremen a pupil of the celebrated Tartini has a most distinguished talent. Her violin is the Lyre of Orpheus in her graceful hands. Her beautifully expressive playing, her style and ease of playing put her in the first rank of virtuosi.

And yet another in *Mercure de France* in September, p. 117, under "Spectacles":

> On the feast of the Assumption a Concert Spirtuel took place . . . M. and Mme de Siremen played a double violin concerto of their own. Mme Siremen is a pupil of the famous Tartini; she has absorbed completely the playing style of this skilled violin master, especially in the handling of complex embellishments for which he is particularly known. It is like a muse touching the Lyre of Apollo and her charming appearance adds still more to the excellence of her musical gifts.

We do not know how many concerts, the Sirmens had been contracted to give, but certainly there was another on 8 September starting with a symphony by Sirmen. This is the only record we have of Lodovico writing a symphony, and alas, the score—if there ever was one—has disappeared. Gaetano Besozzi with Jadin and Molidor played a triple concerto for oboe, bassoon, and cor de chasse; Mme Larrivée sang *Exultate justi* written by Tissier, "a very young composer"; a violin concerto by Sirmen was performed by Mme Lombardini-Sirmen; an Italian air sung by Mlle Fel was accompanied on the oboe by Besozzi; and to finish, *Super flumina* by Giroust.[19]

The reviewers were again very kind. *L'Avant Coureur* wrote on 12 September that "Mme Lombardini Sirmen played a violin concerto by M. Sirmen with a great deal of grace and good taste". And *Mercure de France* in October wrote "Mme de Sirmen enchanted her listeners with the way in which she performed a concerto by her husband. This charming virtuoso draws from her instrument sounds so brilliant and bewitching that they reach the heart".

The Sirmens were still in Paris in December when another concert took place on the 8th with "a concerto by Sirmen played by Mme Lombardini-Sirmen" along with an oboe concerto composed and played by Besozzi.[20] The concert was reviewed in the *Mercure de France* in January 1769, p. 151:

> Mme de Sirmen, from whom we have by now come to expect some new phenomenon in her violin playing, played a concerto written by her husband M. de Sirmen. She is the first of her sex to challenge the success of our great artists. The audience forgot their characteristic French reserve and gave her the thunderous applause she deserved. They recognised the high level of her talent.

A fortnight later on Christmas Eve, Lodovico performed alone a "Symphony by Sirmen" and on the same programme there were two Italian airs "by Barthélémont sung by Mme Barthélémont". Maddalena was to perform with them in London later.

There is then a gap until 13 March the following year when "Mme Lombardini played the violin", the concert ending with *Stabat* by Pergolèse.[21] A week later: "A violin sonata played by Mme Lombardini-Sirmen"—was it one of Tartini's or one of her own?[22] And the final reference to Maddalena is on 25 March: "A new violin concerto played by Mme Lombardni-Sirmen".[23] Again, was it one of her own compositions? The *Mercure de France* continued to be complimentary:

> Mme Lombardini Sirmen, student of the celebrated Tartini
> played some violin concertos and was greatly admired for
> the power of her bow and the delicacy of her playing; she
> is a muse holding Apollo's lyre.[24]

We can also get some idea of Maddalena's playing from Charles
Burney. When he visited Florence in 1770 he went to a concert where
the violinist Pietro Nardini and his pupil, the young Englishman
Thomas Linley, were both soloists:

> Signor Nardini played . . . in such a manner as to leave
> nothing to wish: his tone is even and sweet; not very loud,
> but clear and certain; he has a great deal of expression in
> his slow movements, which it is said, he has happily caught
> from his master Tartini . . . his stile is delicate, judicious,
> and highly finished. Whoever has heard the polished
> performance of the celebrated Signora Sirmen, may form a
> pretty just idea of Signor Nardini's manner of playing.[25]

Although Burney made his long journey in 1770 he did not publish his
journal until 1771, by which time he must have heard Maddalena perform in London.

The *Concert Spirituel* engagements add up to seven concerts in
seven months. Perhaps the Sirmens gave violin lessons as well. After
all, Maddalena must have spent some years teaching the violin to the
younger musicians at the Mendicanti, and probably they also gave private concerts in the homes of the nobility.

While they were in Paris two important events occurred. First on 5
December 1768, before the *Concert Spirituel* performance on 8
December, the privately published edition of Lodovico's first printed
opus was advertised in the Parisian newspaper *Affiches, annonces et
avis divers*:

> Trois trios pour deux violins et basse.

> Six nouveaux trios à deux violins et basse, par Louis
> Sirmen, [1er] violon de la Ste-Chapelle de Bergame. Prix: 7
> Liv. 4,s., chez l'auteur, rue des Grands-Augustins, à l'hôtel
> de Turin, etc.

These trios were published by J.J. Hummel the following year and
stayed in their catalogues until the early nineteenth century. In fact,

they were the only music written by Lodovico to appear in an international catalogue:

> SEI TRII / A Due Violini é Basso, / DEDICATI / A sua Eccelenza / BRANCACCIO / COMTE DI LAURAGUAIS / DA / LODOVICO SIRMEN / Primo Violino, al Attual Servizio; Della Veneranda Capella / di Santa Maria Maggiore / di Bergamo, /OPERA IA, /On peut les avoir a Amsterdam, / chez J.J.HUMMEL, Marchand & Imprimeur de Musique,/ Prix f3.10.

Louis-Léon-Felicité Lauraguais, Duke of Brancas (1733–1824), seems to have been a colourful character. His palace was on the Rue de l'université in the parish of St Sulpice; his mistress was the actress Madeleine-Sophie Arnould. His mother, Dianne Adélaïde de Mailly-Nesle, Duchess of Lauraguais (1714–69), as a child had played with the future King Louis XV. He had a brief military career and then devoted himself to music, literature, and science. He supported artists and intellectuals, including Voltaire, who dedicated his play *l'Ecossaise*, performed in 1760, to him. He wrote *Droit de la France* (Paris 1766–70), resulting in him being imprisoned in the Bastille, and the Châteaux of Dijon, Strasbourg, and Metz. We do not know of any specific connection between Lodovico Sirmen and the Count—perhaps the Sirmens gave concerts in his palace or even taught the Count's children.

The second important event was the publication of:

> Sei Quartetti / a Violino I e II, Viola, e Violoncello / Dedicati/Al Illustrissimo Signor Conte / Benevento / Di Sant. Raffaelle / e Composti da /Lodovico, e Madelena Laura Syrmen. / Prix 9 liv. / Opera III. A Paris / Chez / Madame Bérault Mde de Musique rue de la Comédie française / Faubourg St Germain au Dieu de l'harmonie / Et aux addresses ordinaries / A.P.D.R.

Here we come to a mystery. The quartets seem to be the work of Maddalena, although they were published as being by "Lodovico e Madelena Laura Syrmen". Why the joint authorship? Was it because when a woman married, her property immediately belonged to her husband? If so, presumably it included her compositions. Or, perhaps it was more difficult to get work published by a woman. However, the quartets are the only music published under the couple's joint names, and when the work was reprinted in London by William Napier, it was advertised as "A Set of Quartets by Madam Syrmen".

The title page of the catalogue where the quartets were advertised reads:

> CATALOGUE Des Ouvrages qui se vendant chez Madame Bérault, M^de [de] Musique, Rue et à côté de la comédie Françoise proche de Carfour de Bassie Faubourg St Germain où l'on trouve un assortment général de toutes sortes de Musique Françoise et Italienne.

The quartets are listed above "Haydn IIe". Presumably the dedication of the quartets to Count Benevento di S. Raffaelle was a "thank you" for his help during their time in Turin. A nice touch is that they were published by a woman—Madame Bérault.

We have no facts about Maddalena's life from the final concert in Paris on 25 March 1769 until her first appearance in London on 10 January 1771. We know from the dedication of Lodovico's string trios in 1768 that at that time he described himself as "1er violon de la Ste-Chapelle de Bergame". Did the couple return to Bergamo, and was their daughter Alessandra born during these eighteen months? Or did they continue their concert tour to the Netherlands? This is a possibility, since the title page of Maddalena's *Six String Trios*, privately printed, probably in 1769, proudly states:

> Six / TRIOS / à / Deux VIOLONS et VIOLONCELLO obligé / Dediées / A Son Altesse Royale / MADAME LA PRINCESSE / d'Orange et de Nassau &c. &c. &c. / Composés / Per MADAME LOMBARDINI SIRMEN / Eleve du célèbre Tartini di Padoue. / Ouvre première.

The Trios were then printed by Sieber in Paris, engraved by Madame Sieber, another professional woman, but with no date, and by J.J. Hummel in Amsterdam, and The Hague, where they are advertised in their music catalogue of 1771.

Madame La Princess, Frédérique-Sophie-Wilhelmine of Prussia, a niece of Frederick the Great, had married William V, Prince of Orange and Nassau (1748–1806), in 1767 at the age of sixteen. William was the son of Princess Anne, daughter of George II of England, who had been a pupil of Handel. The court was lively and musical with its own orchestra, and Wilhelmine herself was an accomplished musician. In April 1769, J. C. Bach visited, and presented a new cantata, six new symphonies, a concerto, and a keyboard solo. The court was always kind and generous to visiting artists, and among musicians who had worked there were the oboist John Christian Fischer (1733–1800) with whom Maddalena was to work in London, and the violinist and composer Pietro Locatelli (1693–1764), a native of Bergamo, who worked at Amsterdam *c.* 1730–64. The publisher J. J. Hummel was established in Amsterdam and brought out Maddalena's *Trios* as well as her *Violin Concertos*. Leopold Mozart along with his children, Wolfgang and Nannerl, visited The Netherlands in 1765, and in the following year during celebrations for William V's eighteenth birthday the Hummels published "A Dutch Song on the Installation of His Serene Highness William V, Prince of Orange &c, &c, &c. Set to music by C. E. Graaf, and furnished with eight artful variations by the celebrated young composer J. G. W. Mozart aged 9" (K.24). The young Mozart also wrote a set of keyboard variations for the song *Wilhelmus van Nassau* (K.25), so Maddalena was in good company for her dedication.

The privately printed edition of Maddalena's *Six Trios* had a dedication to Princess Wilhelmina:

Madame

Your Royal Highness has graciously given me permission to dedicate to you the first of my compositions and I regard this as the highest award for acquiring skills not expected of my sex. You are indeed our ornament and glory, Madame, by being judge and protectress of the arts. Since at first I was afraid to pursue such work, I was soon reassured and I hope that Your Royal Highness will accept my work with your characteristic kindness.

Madame, Your Royal Highness, Your very humble and obedient Servant

Lombardini Sirmen

These *Trios* are to be found advertised in the Hummel catalogue for 1771 together with Lodovico's, and both sets remained in print until at least 1814.

We then lose sight of the Sirmens from the notice of their last concert in Paris on 25 March 1769 until early 1771 when Maddalena was to be found in London and Lodovico in Ravenna. By this time they had made the momentous decision to follow separate careers; for Maddalena to continue to lead the life of a virtuoso violinist and composer on the international circuit, and for Lodovico to continue his musical career in Ravenna. But Maddalena did not travel alone. The gossip writer Ippolito Gamba Ghiselli writing in Ravenna in 1777 said, "Signora Sirmen had a Venetian priest with her who always accompanied her in her journeys ever since the first days of her marriage". This was, of course, Giuseppe Terzi.[26]

In September 1770 Maddalena's mother, Gasparina Gambirasi, died in Venice:

28 September 1770

> Signora Gasparina Gambirasi, daughter of the late Antonio Gambirasi and wife of the late Pietro Lombardini, who lived in the Campo dell'Angelo, died at the age of 55 in bed during the day at six in the morning of an illness. She was administered the sacrament of Extreme Unction on 2 September 1770, by the parish priest.[27]

Notes

1. I am indebted to Gloria Eive for this information and translation.
2. Faenza Biblioteca Communale mss. Abbate Cesare Mengolini, *Aggiunta alla Cronaca del Cavaliere Carlo Zanelli, 1766–85*, 11.10.1767.
3. [Anna, Lady Miller], *Letters from Italy to a Friend residing in France by an English Woman* (London 1776), III, 284–85.
4. Samuel Sharp, *Letters from Italy . . . In the years 1765 and 1766* (London, 1767), 274–75.
5. *Tour*, 62–63.
6. *Poole*, 40.
7. *Tour*, 72.
8. Copy in Bologna Conservatorio di Musica G.B. Martini.
9. Sharp, 270–271.
10. Turin, *Ordinati delle Societá del cavalieri*, coll. IX, vol. VI, n. 169, cc 221^v–222^r.
11. Marie-Thérèse Bouquet, *Il Teatro di Corte dalla Origini al 1788, Storia del Teatro Regio di Torino* (Turin: Cassa di Risparmo di Torino, 1976), 319–20.
12. Bologna Conservatorio.
13. Sharp, 190–1.
14. *The Gentleman's Guide to his tour Through Italy* (London, 1887), 195.
15. *Mercure de France* (April 1737).

16. *Pierre*, 114.
17. *Pierre*, 295, no. 829.
18. (London, 1777–89), XIX, 266.
19. *Pierre*, 295, no. 830.
20. *Pierre*, 295, no. 832.
21. *Pierre*, 295, no. 836.
22. *Pierre*, 296, no. 838.
23. *Pierre*, 296, no. 842.
24. *Mercure de France* (April 1769), 143.
25. *Tour*, 184.
26. Ravenna Archivio Storico Communale mss Ghiselli XI, cc. 85^v–78^v.
27. AP Raffaele, *Morti*, Registro 1767–77, *c.* 55^r.

Chapter 6

LONDON (1)

HAY-MARKET

At the King's Theatre in the Hay-market
To morrow will be perform'd a sacred Oratorio, called

GIOAS RE di GIUDA

The Music composed by Mr Bach
the principal parts by Signor Tenducci, Signor Savoi,
Signora
Grassi, Signora Guglielmi, Mrs Barthelemon and
Signor Morigi
End of Act I, a Solo on the Violoncello by Mr Duport.
In the Second
Act, after the duetto, a Concerto on
the violin
by the celebrated Mrs Lombardini Sirmen
And also in the Second Act, a Song by Signora
Guglielmi, accompanied by Mr Duport.
Pit and boxes to be put together, and no Person to
be admitted without tickets, which will be delivered
That Day at the
Office of the Theatre at Half a guinea each.

First Gallery 5s. Second Gallery 3s.
The Galleries, Pit and Boxes to be opened at Five
To begin at Half past six. Vivant Rex & Regina

This was the advertisement to be found in *The Public Advertiser* on 9
January 1771; it was Maddalena's début in England. What were
theatrical and musical conditions like in London then?

London was rich and could afford to import the best instrumentalists, singers, and composers. Why were they better than the home-bred
ones? Probably because there was better teaching available in other
countries—after all, Maddalena must have been superbly taught during
all her years at the Mendicanti and by her beloved Tartini who was
considered the best violin teacher in Europe. Other countries had many
small courts with musical establishments where aspiring musicians
could be educated, whereas England only had the one, the Chapel
Royal. This was in London, and by the eighteenth century it had lost
the importance it had enjoyed in earlier times. But London was
prosperous, the wealthy needed to be entertained, and foreign
musicians willingly came, hoping to make their fortunes. As early as
1713 Johann Mattheson wrote in his *Neu-eröffnetes Orchester* "he who
in the present time wants to make a profit out of music betakes himself
to England. The Italians exalt music; the French enliven it; the
Germans strive after it; the English pay for it well".

In 1761 the King, George III, had married Princess Charlotte of
Mecklenberg-Strelitz. She was only seventeen at the time, had been
educated by Protestant nuns, and did not speak a word of English.
Fortunately, the King spoke German and both of them French, and the
newly married pair soon discovered they both loved the theatre and
music. Until the King's health started to fail, they seem to have led a
very happy and contented life together, going frequently to the theatre
for plays, operas, and concerts. So, theatre-going and musical events
were very fashionable among the "Nobility and Gentry".

Queen Charlotte, like Princess Wilhelmina of Orange, was also kind
to musicians. The Mozarts came to London before they went to the
Netherlands, and on 27 April 1764 from 6 to 9 p.m. they were received
by the King and Queen and given a gift of 24 guineas. Their next concert was on 9 May, a benefit for the cellist Graziani, and we may be
sure their father Leopold was behind the notice in *The Public Advertiser* on 9 May 1764, part of which reads:

Concerto on the Harpsichord by Master Mozart, who is a real Prodigy of Nature; he is but Seven Years of Age, plays any thing at first Sight, and composes amazingly well. He has had the Honour of exhibiting before their Majesties greatly to their Satisfaction.

On 18 January 1765 appeared:

Six Sonatas for the Harpsichord / which can be played with the accompaniment of Violin, or Transverse / Flute Very Humbly dedicated To Her Majesty Charlotte / Queen of Great Britain / composed by I. G. Wolfang Mozart Aged eight Years / Opus III. London. Printed for the Author and Sold at his / Lodgings At Mr Williamson in Thrift Street, Soho.

It had the usual grovelling dedication ending with "Your Majesty's Very humble and very obedient little servant J. G. W. Mozart". And Leopold wrote, "Once I leave England I shall never see guineas again". So Maddalena came to a capital city ruled by a music-loving royal family and where attending musical events was the norm for the aristocracy.

Maddalena can hardly have arrived in England immediately before her first concert on 10 January 1771. She must have been fairly well known in London, already to be billed as "the celebrated Mrs Lombardini Sirmen". G.W. Stone Jr states that in the season of 1770–71 Sga Lombardini Sirmen played the violincello [sic] at the "King's Opera House", but does not state where he found his information.[1] However, this is unlikely since women were able to play in public as soloists but it would have been most unusual to see a woman in the pit. The logical explanation is that she was brought to England partly through an invitation from Johann Christian Bach and partly through the network of ex-pupils of Tartini.

Johann Christian Bach (1735–82) was the youngest son of Johann Sebastian Bach and his second wife, Anna Magdalena. In 1756 he went to Italy and had lessons from Padre Martini at Bologna, eventually becoming a popular composer of operas. In 1762 he came to London as Music Master to Queen Charlotte and tactfully dedicated a set of harpsichord concertos to her, number six ending with variations on "God Save the King". He stayed in London for the rest of his life. Opera could not be staged during Lent, so in 1770 he decided to organize a season of oratorios at the King's Theatre in spite of the fact that there were already oratorios to be heard at Covent Garden and Drury Lane. He included his own oratorio, *Gioas Re di Giuda*, but, as Burney said, "the success, however, was neither flattering nor profitable, though the undertaking was patronised and frequently honoured with the presence of their Majesties".[2] The following year, 1771, there was another performance of *Gioas* on 10 January which included Maddalena Lombardini Sirmen playing a violin concerto, as we have seen in the advertisement on the opening page of this chapter.

Maddalena was immediately among friends. Signora Guglielmi was Lelia Achiapati, her old colleague and fellow violinist at the Mendicanti. After Burney had visited there in 1770 he remarked, "it was here that the two celebrated female performers, the Archiapate, now Signora Guglielmi, and Signora Maddalena Lombardini Sirmen, who have received such great and just applause in England, had their musical instructions".[3] Mrs Barthelemon and Maddalena had shared a concert platform in Paris on 24 December 1768. The soprano, Cecilia Grassi, had sung in Venice in 1760 and was eventually to marry J.C. Bach; Burney, unkind as ever, said of her, "[she] was inanimate on the stage, and far from beautiful in her person".[4] When Bach died in 1782 Cecilia Grassi was left penniless and was only able to go back to Italy with the help of Queen Charlotte and her fellow musicians who gave a benefit concert for her. Angelo Morigi (1725–1801) was a pupil of Tartini. The castrato Giusto Ferdinando Tenducci (*c.* 1736–after 1800) seems to have been a colourful character. He was arrested in England in 1760 because of debts he had left behind in Italy and spent most of that year in prison. *The Public Advertiser* of 13 January 1761 contains a pathetic advertisement asking the public to come to his benefit:

> [he] has been detained in the Prison of the King's Bench
> eight months, great Part of that Time confined to a sick-
> bed, where he must have perished for Want of Necessaries
> and Attendance, had he not been relieved by the Charity of
> the Humane.

And Burney says he "embellished that residence by his talents and amused its inhabitants" and was allowed to accept concert engagements outside the prison "attended by a *garde du corps*", a certain Jewish lady, his patroness "taking him (and presumably the *garde du corps*) to and from the concerts in her carriage". Anyway, in 1771

Tenducci became the "first man" in the opera season and frequently shared a platform with Maddalena.[5]

We do not know whether this performance of *Gioas* on 10 January was a success or not. Other attractions on the same day were David Garrick in *The Suspicious Husband* at Drury Lane and, at Covent Garden, *The English Merchant*. There were further performances of *Gioas* on 16, 17, 23, and 24 January, and we can feel sure that the audiences came to see Maddalena. After all, at that time the violin was not an instrument normally played by a woman; suitable feminine instruments were the harpsichord or the new pianoforte, musical glasses, and the English guitar. Let us hope that the sight of an attractive woman playing the violin with elegance and beauty of tone increased the audiences. To encourage the public to venture out in what seems to have been a cold spell of weather, in *The Public Advertiser* for 17 January we read, "Great care will be taken to have additional fires to make warm the said theatre". On 15 January Mrs Delany, the friend of Handel and a prolific letter-writer, wrote to her friend Mrs Port of Ilam: "Yesterday morning, you had not been gone half an hour when in came my little Lord Warwick to invite you and me to a little concert tomorrow to hear the *fiddling woman*".[6] Isaac Reed (1742–1807), the author and editor of Shakespeare, wrote in his diary for 24 January 1771, "went with Mr Lax and Cruso to the Haymarket, heard part of *Gioas Re di Giuda* and a concerto on the violin by Sig. Sirmin", but that was all he wrote; whether he enjoyed it or not he makes no comment.[7]

We next hear of Maddalena in an advertisement in *The Public Advertiser* for a concert on 8 February:

> For the Benefit and Increase of a FUND / established for the Support of Decayed MUSICIANS / and their FAMI-LIES / At the King's Theatre in the Hay-Market / on Friday the 8th of February will be a grand Concert of / Vocal and Instrumental MUSIC. / By the Opera Singers and Orchestra, and other celebrated Performers / First Act. Overture in the Olimpiade, Song / Sigra Grassi. Song, Sig. Savij, Concerto Bassoon, / Mr Baumgarten. Song, Sigra Guglielmi. Second / Act. Concerto German Flute, Mr Tacet. Song, Sigra / Romani. Song, Sigra Guglielmi. / Solo on the Vio/loncello, Mr Du Port. Song, Sig[ra]. Tenducci. Song, / Sig. Ristorini. Trio in Ezio, composed by Sig. Gugl/ielmi. Third Act. Concerto Hautboy, Mr Fischar. / Song. Sigra Grassi. Song, Sig. Tenducci. Concerto / on the

Violin, Mrs Sirmen. Quartetto in Astarto,/composed by Mr
Bach. A new Full piece, composed / by Sig. Giordani.

The ticket prices were pit and boxes: half a guinea, first gallery: 5s,
upper gallery: 3s 6d. The money will be put to good use:

> for the support of Decayed Musicians and their Families;
> widows of Decayed Musicians, and in maintaining and
> educating Orphans who are left in distress, and in putting
> them Apprentices, and for Physic, burials and other neces-
> sary charges, relating to the Charity the sum of £781.6.8.
> And that the books are open and may be inspected by any
> Gentleman (being a subscriber to the Charity) the first
> Sunday in every month at a Meeting of the Governors at
> the Turk's head in Gerard Street, St Anne's.

Maddalena had obviously been swept into helping the charity along
with many of the other Italian musicians in London at that time. It must
have been a very important social occasion, since a performance of the
oratorio *La Passione* had to be postponed.

On Wednesday, 30 January, we read in *The Public Advertiser*:

ALMACK'S

> SIGNORA SIRMEN begs Leave to acquaint the Nobility
> and Gentry of her Benefit, which upon the Tickets was
> fixed for Friday the 1st of February, is obliged to be post-
> poned; and timely Notice will be given in the Papers of the
> Day on which it is to be.

Poor Maddalena; one wonders what had happened. The benefit concert
was very important to musicians, as a great deal of money could be
made in one night if sufficient people came or, alternately, if the expenses were large and the audiences small, there could be a loss.
Maddalena obviously knew all about benefits. There were so many
events happening in London society that it was as well to book a date
for a benefit as soon as possible, even though the date might have to be
changed if it clashed with another event which could take away the
potential audience. Frequently musicians performed for free at each
other's benefits, and the Italian performers seem to have been particularly generous to one another. As Simon McVeigh says in his invalu-
able book, *Concert Life in London from Mozart to Haydn*:

The promoter was himself responsible for all kinds of minutae: newspaper-advertising, tickets and bills, staging and candles, refreshments for audience and performers, hire and tuning of keyboard instruments. He might have to engage bill-posters, organ-blowers, music-porters, attendants and constables. In 1757 a "Widow under great Misfortunes by Losses at Sea" made a point of promising two doorkeepers "whose Honesty may be relied on" . . . It was quite possible to make a loss on a benefit. In 1760 [the singer] Gambarini advertised a third benefit to recoup the losses from the first two, losses caused by her assumption that unreturned tickets had been bought. Ten years later Barthelemon was plagued with forgery of Marybone tickets.[8]

Permission to hold a concert also had to be given by the Lord Chamberlain. The composer Matthias Vento asked for permission to hold a benefit on 26 April 1773.

I do hereby give Leave and Licence to Mr Mathias Vento to have a concert of Vocal and Instrumental Musick performed for his Benefit on Monday the 26th Instant between the Hours of Eight in the Morning and Four in the Afternoon, at any of the Theatres or Concert Rooms within the City or Liberties of Westminster. Given under my hand and Seal this Sixteenth Day of April 1773 In the Thirteenth Year of His Majesty's Reign. (Signed) Hertford.[9]

Let us hope that Giuseppe Terzi was able to look after all these details for Maddalena and that her fellow Italian musicians rallied round to help.

Cecilia Grassi had had a benefit the previous year, and her advertisement asked:

the kind Protection of the Nobility and Gentry, and hopes the subscribers to the boxes will not think her remiss in not waiting on them in person, she being a Stranger in the Method how to proceed, therefore most humbly desires that they will send their orders to the Office of the said Theatre.[10]

Johann Christian Bach and Carl Friedrich Abel had started a series of highly fashionable subscription concerts. They were first held at the house of Mrs Cornelys in Carlisle House, Soho Square. She was a singer, born in Venice (1723–97), and after a singing career throughout Europe (Casanova said "her good fortune had not depended entirely on her talent") she rented, then bought Carlisle house. It is said she was helped by Elizabeth Chudleigh, maid to the Princess of Wales until she was dismissed for bigamy in 1776. Mrs Cornelys started Wednesday Subscription concerts and promised her patrons "Tea below stairs, and ventilators above [whereby] the present complaints of excessive heat will be obviated".

As Charles Burney wrote:

> Bach and Abel uniting interests, opened a subscription, about 1763, for a weekly concert, and as their own compositions were new and excellent, and the best performers of all kinds which our capital could supply, enlisted under their banners, this concert was better patronised and longer supported than perhaps any one had ever been in this country; having continued for full twenty years with uninterrupted prosperity.[11]

In 1768 the concerts were moved to Almack's rooms in King Street, between St James's Street and St James's Square, and that is where Maddalena was to have her benefit. Here is a typical advertisement for a concert there:

ALMACK'S

> Mess Bach and Abel beg Leave to acquaint the Nobility and Gentry, Subscribers to their CONCERTS, That the Sixth will be on Wednesday next, under the Direction, for that Night of Mr BACH.
>
> No person will be admitted without Tickets, and no Tickets but those of the Night will be admitted.
>
> The tickets are transferable as usual, Ladies to Ladies, and Gentlemen to Gentlemen only. The Ladies Tickets are blue and the Gentlemen's yellow.
>
> The Nobility and Gentry are desired to be particular to order their coachmen to set them down at the usual Door with the Horses Heads towards St James's Street; and to take them up in the like Manner at the next Door near the Square, as the other Door will be only for the Chairs.
>
> The doors to be opened at six, and to begin at Seven.[12]

So London had its traffic problems even in the eighteenth century. The names of the performers were never given in the newspaper advertisements, but it is highly likely that Maddalena would have played at some of the Bach–Abel concerts. In 1767 Bach opened an account at Drummond's Bank (now the Bank of Scotland), and on 17 May 1771 Sig. Sirmen was paid £105 by Bach.[13] Unfortunately, the document does not say why the money was paid, but it must have been for playing at concerts; the amount was obviously 100 guineas (a guinea was £1 1s), a common way to pay fees even until fairly recently. The singer Cecilia Grassi was also paid 100 guineas the following year.

Saturday, 9 February 1771, must have been a very exciting day for Maddalena, for the announcement of the first publication of any of her music in England appeared in *The Public Advertiser*:

> NEW MUSIC / this Day is published, / The First Act of the Opera Semiramide; / composed by Sig. Cocchi, Price 3s 6d. Six / Concertos in 8 Parts by Barthelemon, 10s 6d. / Twelve Divertiments for two Guittars, or a Guittar / and Violin, composed by Sig. Merchi, 6s. Six / Divertiments, by Sig. Comi, for the Harpsichord, 1s 6d. / A favourite Overture, by Bach, 3s. A Treatise on / Singing, by Dr Nares, 3s 6d. The celebrated Sig-/nora Sirmen's Trios, 10s 6d. / Printed by Welcker, in Gerrard Street, St Ann's / Soho. / N.B. a new work will be publish'd every Week / during this Season, by Welcker.

Similar advertisements for the Hummel edition of the *Six Trios* appeared in the Parisian papers, *L'Avant Coureur* on 18 March and in the *Affiches, annonces et avis divers*, on 21 March.

Maddalena was busy again on 15 February, playing at the King's Theatre in the Haymarket "a solo and Concerto on the Violin" during a performance of *Judas Maccabaeus* "Composed by Mr Handel" and the following day performing the same during *Messiah*. Soloists usually played their own compositions at concerts, so her concertos were getting a good airing in London. Evening performances seem very long to us. At a concert on 7 March there was the first part of the oratorio *La Passione* by Jomelli followed by a concerto from Maddalena, Pergolesi's *Stabat Mater*, a bassoon concerto by Mr Baumgarten, a violin solo from Maddalena, and to end "a Grand Chorus by Signor Guglielmi". There is, also, a curious ending to the advertisement: "By their MAJESTIES Command No person Whomsoever to be admitted behind the scenes, or into the Orchestra".

Poor Maddalena does not seem to have had much luck with her benefit. On 4 March 1771 in *The Public Advertiser* under "AL-MACKS" we read, "Signora Sirmen begs leave to acquaint the Nobility and Gentry that her Benefit which upon the tickets was fixed for This Day, is obliged to be postponed; and timely notice will be given in the Papers of the Day on which it is to be". She seems to have performed on average at least twice a week during the season from January to the end of May, and the first time she took part in a benefit concert was on 21 March, "For the Benefit of Signor and Signora Guglielmi". Guglielmi was a very prolific composer, writing operas, oratorios, instrumental and sacred works, and for their benefit they gave a performance of one of Guglielmi's most successful operas, *I Viaggiatori Ridicoli*. It was to be another long evening: "The favourite comic opera *I Viaggiatori Ridicoli*" by Guglielmi himself, with a cello concerto by Cirri at the end of the first act, an oboe concerto by Fisher at the end of the second, and a violin concerto by Maddalena at the end of the third.

At last, on Saturday, 15 April, Maddalena had her benefit. She clearly believed in advertising. As a keen businesswoman with her nose for publicity she put notices of her benefit concert in *The Public Advertiser* no fewer than fifteen times where "advertisements of a moderate length" cost 3s each. Let us hope she recouped her considerable outlay. It was obviously going to be a very grand occasion:

> ALMACK'S / For the Benefit of Signora SIRMEN / On Monday 15 April will / be a / GRAND CONCERT / Under the direction of Mess. Bach and Abel / The Vocal Parts by Sig. Guadagni, Instrumental by / Mr Wendling, (first German Flute to his S.A.S. / L'Electeur Palatin) and Mess. Fisher, Cirri, and / other principal performers, Signora Sirmen will play / a Concerto on the Harpsichord. / Tickets 10s 6d to / be had of Signora Sirman, at no. 36 / in Suffolk Street, near the Haymarket; at Welcher's Music Shop on Ger/ard Street, Soho; and at Almack's, Pall Mall. Tickets / Delivered for the 1st of February will be admitted.

The intriguing thing about this notice is the fact that Maddalena was going to play a harpsichord concerto. There was no reason not to, because, at the Mendicanti she had studied violin, harpsichord, and singing. The following year the publication of Maddalena's violin concertos started in England and in February 1773 they were published in a version adapted for the harpsichord by Tommaso Giordani. Did she play one or more of these arrangements? It would have been good publicity. The soloists were all well-known performers, especially the castrato Gaetano Guadagni (c. 1725–92), who had sung for Handel. An anonymous admirer wrote to the printer of the *Town and Country Magazine*:

> to hear the sweet GUADAGNI warble his thrilling airs, melts one into such extasy nothing can equal. Oh! that charming creature . . . Had I the riches of Peru I would bestow them upon him for an hour's charming conversation blended with the ductlike quavers of his dear, dear pipe.[14]

There was another charity concert; the oratorio *Ruth* by Felice Giardini in aid of the Lock Hospital where venereal diseases were treated. The following notice was placed in *The Public Advertiser*; as ever, putting on concerts has never been easy:

> LONDON Lock Hospital, 20 April 1771
>
> The Governors of this Hospital being obliged to change the Day for the Performance of their Oratorio *Ruth*, on account of the prior Engagement of some of the principal Performers on the 25th instant which did not occur to them at the Time they promised to perform for the Benefit of the Charity; it is now fixed for Saturday next.

Giardini himself was playing first violin and "After Part the Second a Concerto on the violin by Signora Sirmen".

Felice Giardini (1716–96), composer and violinist, came to England in 1750. Charles Burney wrote:

> His first public performance in London, at which I was present . . . [he] played a solo and concerto, though there was very little company, the applause was so loud, long and furious, as nothing but that bestowed on Garrick had ever equalled. I had met him the night before at a private concert, with Guadagni and Frasi, at the house of Napthali Franks Esq. . . . when, besides solos of his own composition of the most brilliant kind, he played several of Tartini's in manuscript.[15]

So we may imagine that Maddalena also was invited to play at private concerts. It was obviously the fashion among certain noble ladies, and Burney is quite amusing about them:

> Given by Mrs Fox Lane, afterwards Lady Bingley, on the arrival of Giardini in England . . . As Giardini was seldom to be heard in public after his arrival, she invited very select parties of the first people in the kingdom to hear him at her house, for which happiness she did not suffer them to remain ungrateful at his benefit . . . the difficulty, or rather impossibility of hearing these professors and illustrious dilettanti anywhere else, stimulated curiosity so much, that there was no sacrifice or mortification to which fashionable people would not submit, in order to obtain admission.[16]

Two days after the performance of *Ruth*, the oboist, Mr Fisher, also had a benefit concert at the Theatre Royal "under the Direction of Mess. Bach and Abel", where Maddalena played a violin concerto.

The end of the Season was in sight, so everybody seemed to be having a benefit. The next was for Mr Kammell on 9 May. He, like Maddalena, had been a pupil of Tartini and had made his London début on 6 May 1768. The programme for his benefit included "a double concerto for two violins; Obligato by Madam Sirmen, and Mr Kammell; with several new pieces by the best composers. Tickets 10s 6d each to be had at Mr Kammell's house in Half Moon Street, Piccadilly." The following season Maddalena's address was Half Moon Street; one wonders if they shared a house. On 14 May *La Schiava* by Piccini was performed at the King's Theatre where "in the last Act a new Song by Signor Giordani to be sung by Signora Ristorini and accompanied by the celebrated Signora Sirmen on the Violin". And on 15 May:

> For the Benefit of Mr Duport . . . [with] a concerto on the Violin by Signora Sirmen . . . N.B. The above Benefit was obliged to be transposed to this Day on account of the Nobility's Mask'd Ball when they humbly hope for the Protection of the Nobility and Gentry.

On Friday, 17 May, "The Last Night of the Subscription for this Season", there was to be *Orfeo* at the King's Theatre. It had been performed for the first time in London the previous year, and it is worth quoting from the programme since Maddalena was to sing in it in 1773:

> The Music as originally composed by Signor GLUCH, to which, in order to make the Performance of a necessary length for an evening's entertainment, Signor BACH has very kindly condescended to add of his own composition all such choruses, airs, and recitatives, as are marked with inverted commas, except those which are sung by Signora *Guglielmi*, and they are likewise an entire new production of Signor GUGLIELMI, her husband.[17]

On 17 May 1771, there were to be "New Dances, Cloaths and Scenes intermixed with Grand Choruses, End of the first act a Concerto on the Violin by the celebrated Signora Sirmen". There had been previous performances of *Orfeo* that season, but the cast lists do not include Maddalena. On Saturday, 25 May, the gentleman astronomer Edward Pigott (1753–1825) went to see *Orfeo*. He wrote in his diary:

> *Orfeo* (pasticcio) at the King's Theatre, with Gaetano Guadagni in the title role and Signora Lombardini Sirmen (violin). Dined with Mr Ratcliffe at the Tavern. Went together to Orfeo the Italian opera—was not pleased— Guadagni the best singer Indifferent—women singers worse—Dancing wretched—better at Caen. The whole in every respect much Inferior to the operas before I left England except the orchestra which is Excellent—madame Sirmen a foreigner Played a concerto on the violin admirably well.[18]

And on 28 May there was at the King's Theatre:

> "La BUONA FIGLIUOLA / the Music by Signor Piccini . . . with dances, / A new dance by a new principal dancer lately arrived from France / with the Hornpipe Dance on Skates, with new Cloaths / . . . In the last Act a new song by Signor Giordani, to be sung / by Signora Ristorini, and accompanied by the celebrated / Signora Sirmen on the violin, being her last performance / this season on this stage.

La Buona Figliuola had been performed several times that season but with no mention of Maddalena. The "Nobility and Gentry" were being coaxed to see the opera again by all the new items—the hornpipe on skates together with Maddalena. The King's Theatre was obviously trying hard to get an audience. So, as far as we know, after this concert Maddalena returned to Italy. Two of her colleagues put a polite notice in *The Public Advertiser*:

Suffolk Street, No. 33, 25 June 1771

Signora Ristorini and Signor Zanca return their sincerest thanks to the Nobility and Gentry for their Indulgences and Encouragement which their endeavours have been favoured with to please the Public thro' this Season. In two or three days after the Expiration of their Engagements with the Managers they go to leave this Kingdom, and thereafter desire that all Persons may apply in due Time to receive their full demands for such bills as are not yet delivered in.

And in October in the same newspaper we read:

HAY-MARKET

King's Theatre, 1 Oct. 1771

The MANAGER requests the Nobility and Gentry, Subscribers to the Operas for the ensuing season, will please to pay their subscriptions to Messrs John Drummond and Co., Bankers at Clay Cross . . . to have their tickets ready to deliver before the operas begin, which will be on the Second of November next.

But there was another mention of Maddalena in *The Public Advertiser* on 8 August:

This Day is published / In Italian and English, Price 1s. / A Letter from the late Sig TARTINI / to Signora MADDALENA LOMBARDINI / now Signora SIRMEN containing important In/structions to Performers on the Violin / Translated by Dr. BURNEY / from the Original / Published at Venice 1770 / Printed for R. Bremner, opposite Somerset House / in the Strand.

All in all, 1771 had been a most exciting year for Maddalena. She had had a very successful London season and her *Six Trios* had been published by Hummel in Amsterdam, Welcker in London, and Sieber in Paris.

Meanwhile, what had been happening to Lodovico? He seems to have become well established in Ravenna, and at the same time that Maddalena was entrancing London with her playing, on 7 April 1771 he was directing an orchestra at S. Maria in Porto where he also played a concerto.[19] The following year on 25 February, Count Marco Fantuzzi wished to thank the Cardinal Legate for help given him in a legal case between the Commune and four abbeys, so:

> he offered him [the Cardinal Legate] a solemn and costly
> *accademia* in the senatorial palace; after the cantata and the
> poetry all the nobility were invited to sumptuous and
> plentiful refreshments. This very noble *accademia* was
> paid for by the noblemen themselves and took place on 25
> February. Domenico Lovatelli made an eloquent and
> impressive speech in praise of the Cardinal. The cantata
> was written by the author of these memoirs [Ghiselli] and
> the music was composed by our celebrated violinist Lodo-
> vico Sirmen. It was played by Sebastiano Emiliani and
> Pietro Gherardi, the first a virtuoso of the Bavarian Elector,
> the second a nephew of our famous Lorenzo Gherardi,
> perhaps better known as "Schiampetta". The Cardinal
> presided over the celebrations and sat on the throne . . .
> The hall was decorated and candle-lit: it shone as bright as
> day. A ball followed which lasted until the early hours.[20]

The libretto of the cantata states:

> CANTATA / PER LA SOLENNE ACCADEMIA /
> TENUTASI DA SIGNORI INFORMI / IL DI XXV
> FABRAJO / DELL'ANNO MDCCLXXII / IN ONORE /
> DEL SIG. CARDINALE / VITALIANO / BORROMEO /
> BENEFICENTISSIMO LEGATO / DI RAVENNA. / IN
> RAVENNA / PER L'EREDE DEL LANDI / CON LIC.
> DE'SUP.

> #### INTERLOCUTORI

> TEMPO. Il Sig. Sebastiano Emiliani Ravennate all'attual
> servizio di Sua Altezza Serma Elettorale di Baviera.

> RAVENNA. Il Sig. Pietro Gherardi Ravennate.

> La Poesia é del Nob. Sig. Conte Ippolito Gamba Ghiselli
> Assessore dell'Accademia.

> La Musica é del celebr. Sig. Lodovico Sirmen Ravennate.[21]

The following year, 8 August 1773, Lodovico was invited to Rimini to direct an orchestra in the Cathedral for the feast of S. Antonio, so the careers of husband and wife were proceeding successfully.

Notes

1. *Stone*, 1497.
2. *History* IV, 497.
3. *Tour*, 184.
4. *History* IV, 491–92.
5. His troubles were far from ended; see Angus Heriot, *The Castrati in Opera* (London: Secker and Warburg, 1956), 185–89.
6. Lady Llanover, ed., *The Autobiography and Correspondence* (London, 1861–62), I, 322.
7. Folger Shakespeare Library, Washington, D.C.
8. Simon McVeigh, *Concert Life in London from Mozart to Haydn* (Cambridge: Cambridge University Press, 1993), 177.
9. London, Public Records Office, Miscellanea, Warrant Books General 1753–93 LC 5/162.
10. *PA*, 10 May 1770.
11. *History* IV, 676.
12. *PA*, 1 March 1773.
13. I am grateful to Simon McVeigh for this information.
14. *Town and Country Magazine*, III (March 1771), 151.
15. *History* IV, 522.
16. *History* IV, 671.
17. G.G. Bottarelli and others, eds., British Library Opera Programme Books, 11714 aa, 21/5.
18. Pigott's diary is in the James Osborn Collection in the Beinecke Library at Yale University.
19. Ravenna, Archivio di Stato, CRS Porto n. 1433, 196.
20. *Ghiselli* I, 44–46.
21. A copy of this document was found in Jane Berdes' papers, but with no source given.

Chapter 7

LONDON (2)

Maddalena Lombardini Sirmen returned to London for a second season in 1772. We say "returned" although we do not know whether she ever left England, but we assume she went back to Italy to see her husband and daughter. Her address was in the newly fashionable area of Half Moon Street off Piccadilly, whereas in 1771 she had lodged at 36 Suffolk Street, close to the Haymarket. Was she sharing a house with Mr Kammell? Even now if you walk around Shepherd Market at the end of Half Moon Street, you can get an idea of the area in the eighteenth century.

The first time Maddalena appears in 1772 is in an advertisement for another concert "For the Benefit and Increase of a Fund established for the Support of Decayed MUSICIANS and their FAMILIES" to be held at the King's Theatre in the Haymarket on Friday, 14 February. The Governors reported that from June 1770 to June 1771 they had spent £826 17s 3d. The programme was similar to that of the previous year, with the singers Signora Guglielmi, Signora Boschetti, Signor Savoi, and Signor Morigi and the instrumentalists Duport, Fisher, Penta, Tacet, and Maddalena playing a violin concerto. The concert actually had to be postponed until 21 February because of the death of the Princess Dowager of Wales; all theatres were closed 8–17 February. This season Maddalena appears to have played in fewer concerts and is advertised as "Signora Sirmen" rather than "the celebrated", but she probably continued to play at private concerts, since by now she must have been an established favourite performer.

Another way of making money, of course, was by private teaching. Teaching music was quite respectable. Mortimer's *London Universal Directory* (1763) lists Masters and Professors of Music, among whom we find "Burney, Charles, Organist" and "Giardini, Signor Felice di, Composer, teaches singing, and the Harpsichord Greek Street, Soho".[1] Advertisements for the teaching of music can be found, such as the following from *The Public Advertiser* of 7 March 1771:

> The harpsichord taught in a very easy and expeditious manner by a Person of undoubted Abilities, who has learned of the most eminent Masters in the Town; will engage to make the Learner play two or three pieces of Music at the End of the Month, and be so far accomplished in twelve months, as to play a Concerto in Concert, on the moderate terms of one guinea a month.

Burney commanded very high fees. We have a receipt for Burney's lessons to Miss Hoare, dated 30 September 1779. The total sum being £40 5s 6d made up of £6 3s for music (Schubert, Eichner, and J.C. Bach sonatas, Vauxhall overtures, harpsichord duets, and a blank music book), £4 4s as the entrance fee, and fifty-seven lessons at half a guinea each.[2]

Already on 17 February Maddalena was advertising her benefit to be held on 23 March at the Theatre Royal in the Haymarket, not at Almack's as the previous year. Had she fallen out with J.C. Bach? On 6 March there was *Messiah* at the Theatre Royal, Covent Garden, where at the end of the first part there was a "Concerto on the French Horn by Mr Ponta (Musician to His Serene Highness the Elector of Mentz)", and Maddalena played a violin concerto at the end of the second part. *The Public Advertiser* on 6 March under "London" reports:

> We hear that uncommon pains have been taken to render the Oratorios at Covent Garden Theatre this season worthy the Attention of the Public, the best performers, vocal and Instrumental having been engaged for that purpose. Two gentlewomen who have never before made their Appearance in Public will sing in the Sacred Oratorio of the *Messiah* this evening. Mr Ponta whose Excellence and singular Execution on the French Horn has been so much

admired, is also retained; as are Signora Sirmen and Mr
Duport to perform on the violin and violoncello.

We have an account of this performance by the writer and composer
John Potter (*c.* 1734–after 1813). He wrote anonymous reviews in *The
Public Ledger* which were collected and printed as "THE / THEATRI-
CAL REVIEW / or /New Companion to the Play-House / CON-
TAINING / A Critical and Historical Account of every TRAGEDY,
COMEDY, OPERA, FARCE &c. exhibited at the Theatres during the
last season . . . By a Society of GENTLEMEN, Independent of Mana-
gerial Influence . . . London 1772". They were actually all written by
John Potter himself. About this performance of *Messiah* he begins:

> The Words of this Oratorio are taken from Holy Writ, and
> the Music is so admirably adapted to the solemnity of the
> design, as to beggar all description: however, we have se-
> lected what has been said of it by several ingenious
> Writers, with some Anecdotes relative to this Oratorio wor-
> thy notice, for the entertainment of our Readers.[3]

He gives a long and fascinating description about how the work came
to be written and its connection with the Foundling Hospital. He goes
on to say:

> Of this wonderful performance, we cannot help observing,
> that there are great inequalities in it; and as the subject is so
> very sacred, the music is of course very solemn; from
> which cause, many of the songs are insufferable tedious
> and heavy; but taking it altogether, it is superior in all
> probability to any thing ever executed by the art of man. In
> the chorusses he has given innumerable instances of an un-
> bounded genius. In short, there is such a sublimity in many
> of the effects he has worked up by the combination of
> instruments and voices, that they seem to be rather the
> effect of inspiration than of knowledge in Music . . . till in
> the winding up of the *Amen*, the ear is filled with such a
> glow of harmony, as leaves the mind in a kind of heavenly
> extasy.[4]

He then mentions the two instrumental soloists, Sirmen and Duport,
but without any criticism of their playing. However, the account of the
performance of Handel's *Judas Maccabaeus* at Covent Garden on 11
March ends with:

> End of the second part, a *Concerto* on the *Violin*, by Signora *Lombardini Sirmen*.—As this celebrated Lady has been some time in *England*, her abilities are pretty generally known. Her tone, and stile of playing is very pleasing, and her execution truly chaste, without any of those unnecessary and extravagant liberties, which the generality of *Solo* players on the *Violin* too frequently give into.[5]

The following day, 12 March, we find in *The Public Advertiser*:

> NEW MUSIC / This day are published / Six solos by Lewis Borghi printed and sold by William Napier at his music shop the corner of Lancaster Court in the Strand near Charing Cross / Where may be had, just published a Set of Trios by Celionati: and six by Windling. NB In this set are several solos, which Mme Syrmen has frequently performed with great applause, particularly that one which gave such universal satisfaction at the Concert in the Opera House for the Benefit of Decayed Musicians.

Then on 18 March:

> For the Benefit of Signora Sirmen. At the Theatre Royal in the Haymarket the 23 instant will be a grand concert of VOCAL and INSTRUMENTAL MUSIC. The vocal part by Signora Grassi; a Concerto on the Oboe by Mr Fisher; Concerto Violoncello Signor Cirri; Concerto French Horn, Mr Ponta; a Concerto German Flute Mr Tacet; a solo etc. by Madam Sirmen.

One hopes that Maddalena was "taken up" by members of the nobility. Burney again about Mrs Lane:

> Whenever a benefit was in contemplation for one of her *protegés*, taking care of the honour of her guests, she obliged them to behave with due gratitude and munificence on the occasion. "Come!" would she say often to her friends, "give me five guineas,"—a demand as implicitly obeyed as if made on the road. Nor had any one, who ever wished to be admitted into such good company again, the courage to ask the occasion of the demand; but patiently awaited the lady's pleasure to tell them whether they should be honoured with a ticket for Giardini's or Mingotti's benefit.[6]

Maddalena took part in more oratorios: another *Messiah*, *Samson* (Handel), and, to quote Potter again:

> THE RESURRECTION / an Oratorio / The Music composed by Mr Arnold. This is a very noble Piece of Composition: the Airs are pleasing, and the Choruses majestically grand; upon the whole this is the most capital Performance in the Oratorio style, Mr *Arnold* has produced . . . End of the second Part, a new *Concerto* on the *Violin*, by Signora *Lombardini Sirmen*, composed by Signor *Cirri*.[7]

This concerto was repeated at a performance of *Abimelech*, also by Mr Arnold, on 25 March.[8] Perhaps it was time to try out something new to tempt the "nobility and gentry". Potter again:

> COVENT GARDEN THEATRE, 27 March / A CONCERTO SPIRITUALE, / In the manner of an Oratorio. / This is a species of entertainment, borrowed from our Volatile Neighbours on the continent, and never performed in *England* before; that is, not directly in this manner.—This Performance was divided into three Parts; the first consisted of Mr *Addison's* celebrated *Hymn*, set to Music by Mr *Handel*, which is a masterly Performance; the second contained *Miserere mei Deus* &c. the Music composed by Signor *Pergolesi*; this is a noble Performance; the third Part consisted of a very fine *Anthem*, by Signor *Nigri of Milan*, a Work of great merit. A *Concerto* on the *French Horn* by Mr *Ponta*; and a *Concerto* on the *Violin* by Signora *Lombardini Sirman*.[9]

But on Monday, 30 March, Mr Fisher had a benefit. Whereas in the previous year it was Maddalena who was the violin soloist, this year it was "*First Violin* and Solo by Linley Jr, from Bath". Was her star quality beginning to fade? The audiences always wanted something new. This was Thomas Linley (1756–78), who must have been about fifteen at the time and already an experienced soloist. He had studied the violin in Italy with Tartini's pupil Nardini and had become friendly with the young Mozart while in Florence in 1770. He was an excellent composer but, alas, was drowned when on holiday at Grimsthorpe castle.

The Concerto Spirituale must have been a success since there was a second one on 8 April. On 3 April *The Public Advertiser* wrote under "London":

> The Concerto Spirituale, performed at the Theatre Royal Covent Garden in the Manner of an Oratorio on Friday last, met with universal approbation; and, by particular Desire, another collection of celebrated Pieces of Music, under the same title, will be performed at the same theatre on Wednesday next. In this second Concerto Spirituale will be introduced Milton's Morning Hymn; the music by PICCINI, JOMELLI, PERGOLESI, CARISSIMI &c.

Maddalena repeated Cirri's Violin concerto, and Potter tells us that

> the *Miserere mei Deus* &c. composed by Signor *Galuppi*. This celebrated Composition is performed in the *Holy Week*, in the Hospital of Incurables at *Venice*. This is the *Miserere* so particularly mentioned by Dr *Burney*, in his Account of the *Present State of Music* in *France* and *Italy*, lately published. The melodies of the Airs are pleasing, the choruses grand, and the Composer has shewn great Taste and Invention in the conduct of the whole.[10]

So, there was even a third "Concerto Spirituale" on 10 April, where, to quote Potter again, part III consisted of:

> "*Dixit Dominus*, by Signor *Pergolesi, with a Concerto on the Violin*, by Signora *Lombardini Sirmen*, being the last time of her performing in *England*.

> We cannot quit this article without remarking, to the credit of the Managers at this Theatre, that there probably never was an evening Performance of so great a variety; however, the great applause the whole received evinced, that the Audience were sensible of an attentive endeavour to please, and, as such signified their approbation.[11]

One wonders when Maddalena left England—if, of course, she did, since on 7 May under "NEW MUSIC" in *The Public Advertiser* we read:

> This Day are published Six Sonatas for the harpsichord, or Piano Forte with Accompaniments composed by Schrieter. Price 10s 6d. Printed and sold by William Napier, at his

Music Shop, the Corner of Lancaster Court, Strand, near
Charing Cross. Where may be had just published, Two
Concertos by Madam Syrmen 3s 6d each. Six quartettos
by Vachon, 10s 6d. Six solos by Borghi, 7s 6d. Six trios by
Windling 7s 6d. Six by Celionati 5s.

Maddalena returned to London for the 1773 season—but, as a singer.
Why? We do not know. Was it that singers then as now were more
highly paid than instrumentalists? Burney said that in the 1770s
Lucrezia Agujari was engaged by the Pantheon in London "at the
enormous salary of £100 a night for singing two songs only!".[12] Or
was she afraid her star billing was now being taken over by others?
Also, dancers became increasingly important, especially Mlle Heinel
and her partner, Fierville. To quote Burney:

> At this time crowds assembled at the Opera-house more for
> the gratification of the eye than the ear; for neither the in-
> vention of a new composer, nor the talents of new singers
> attracted the public to the theatre, which was almost aban-
> doned until the arrival of Mademoiselle Heinel, whose
> extraordinary merit had an extraordinary recompense; for
> besides the £600 salary allowed her by the Hon. Mr.
> Hobart as manager, she was complimented with a *regallo*
> of six hundred more from the Macaroni Club . . . Cocchi
> the composer said "It is very extraordinary, that the English
> set no value upon anything but what they pay an exorbitant
> price for".[13]

Or was it that Signora Guglielmi—Lelia Achiapati—and her husband
had left England and there was the need for another soprano?
Maddalena had been trained as a singer in the Mendicanti, so there was
no reason why she should not sing professionally. After all, at the
Mendicanti, Lelia as well as a singer had been a violin pupil of Antonia
Cubli, who had been taught by Tartini. Anyway, Burney was very
scathing about Maddalena as a singer in his *History*, but then he
frequently was about many musicians. Here is what he wrote:

> In *Sofonisba* and the *Cid* MADAME SYRMEN, the
> scholar of Tartini, who was so justly admired for her
> polished and expressive manner of playing the violin, ap-
> peared as a singer, in the part of second women; but having
> been *first woman* so long upon her instrument, she de-
> graded herself by assuming a character in which, though

not destitute of voice and taste, she had no claim to superi-
ority.[14]

In any case, the year, and Maddalena's new career, started well. On
19 January 1773 Maddalena took the part of Elvyra in Antonio Maria
Sacchini's opera *Il Cid* with a libretto by Giovan Gualberto Bottarelli.
Sacchini (1730–86), a composer of *opere serie*, had been *Maestro di
Coro* at the Derelitti (Ospedaletto) in Venice from 1768 to 1773. The
other singers in the opera were Ristorini, Millico, Savoi, Micheli, and
Signora Girelli-Aguilar. *Il Cid* was performed about twenty times
between 19 January and 19 June 1773, and Burney said the production
was "full of taste, elegance, and knowledge of stage effects".[15] The
advertisements make no mention of the singers, but on 23 January the
audience was offered:

> The music, entirely new, composed by Sig. Sacchini with
> Dances between the Acts, intermixed with grand Choruses.
> End of the Opera a Grand Serious Ballet, with a Pas de
> Deus and a Grand Chaconne, by Mlle Heinel, Mons.
> Fierville, and other Principal dancers with new Cloaths and
> new decorations.

So we can see that it was the dancers who would attract the audience.
The Westminster Magazine in a review in January said:

> The composer has been more successful than the editor.
> Signor Sacchini has exerted a happy genius in the composi-
> tion and arrangement of the music. The choruses are grand
> throughout; and indeed the various situations which occur
> in the piece are illustrated by characteristic graces of the
> music. The managers too have done their duty. In the
> dresses, magnificence has been studied; and elegance in the
> scenery and other decorations. On the whole, let us forget
> that this piece is nonsense, and the rest will be agreeable.
> Let the judgement be lulled asleep, and the eye and ear will
> be satisfied.[16]

And the *Macaroni and Theatrical Magazine* said in the issue of
October 1772–September 1773

> The music, which is excellent merited all the applause it
> received, and does additional credit to Signor Sacchini as a
> composer. The audience were so particularly pleased with
> many of the airs, that they encored them *three times*, a

practice without derogating from either the merit of the performer, or composer, we must unhesitatingly condemn, as it loads the piece with too great a sameness, as well as makes it unnecessarily long.

On the other hand:

> A new Opera, called *Il Cid* was represented this month at the King's Theatre in the Haymarket. This, deformed and monstrous as it appears to be, is no other than the *Cid* of Corneille, which was first transformed into an Opera by a dull abbot at Rome (his name Spizzi). Signor *Bottarelli* is the editor of the present Opera, but has walked too closely in the footsteps of Spizzi to be successful. He has infused into his Opera more numerous graces than Spizzi possessed, but has preserved all his absurdities. The truth is, the genius of Corneille towers above common mortals, and imitation cannot reach it; his sentiment, his expression, his manner, are much too sublime to be chanted by eunuchs, and twisted into cantatas.[17]

Reading through the advertisements for *Il Cid*, it seems extraordinary that the singers are never mentioned, whereas the dances seem to be changed for almost every performance. On 26 January there was "a *pastoral Dance* by Leppie"; on 2 February, "End of Opera: A New Grand Historical Ballet entitled *L'Isle Desert*"; on 16 February, "an *Allemande*"; 20 February, "*Grand Serious Ballet* and *Chaconne* by Mlle Heinel &c., a *Grand Ballet* intermix'd with *Grand Choruses, Pastoral Dance, New Allemande*", and so it goes on. It must have been an extremely popular evening out to warrant so many performances.

The Public Advertiser announced on 30 January "NEW MUSIC / NB In a few days will be published Madam Sirmen's Concertos, adapted for the harpsichord by Sig. Giordani". Then on 1 March under NEW MUSIC:

> This day are published MADAM Syrmen's concertos, adapted for the Harpsichord by Sig. Giordani, Price 7s. 6d. With accompanyments Price £1.1s. . . . Printed for and sold by William Napier, at his Music shop, the Corner of Lancaster Court, Strand, near Charing Cross.

So far we have found no newspaper advertisements for Maddalena appearing in Gluck's *Orfeo*. However, in *The General Evening Post* for 9–11 March under "Opera Intelligence" we read:

> the celebrated Opera of *Orfeo*, in two acts; Millico and Girelli were extremely capital in the last Act . . . The sweet Syrman gave great pleasure in her character, some of her best songs however were left out, which was a palpable detriment to the performance.[18]

We also have two accounts of the same incident during a perform-ance, the first in a letter from Mrs Harris to her son in Berlin[19] and a rather longer account by R.J.S. Stevens in manuscript in the University Library, Cambridge. He was a sixteen-year-old music student when he saw a performance in 1773:

> Signora Syrmen was a celebrated Performer on the Violin when in London. After the novelty of her appearance as an instrumental performer had subsided, she appeared as a secondary *singer* on the Italian Opera Stage . . . I was at the Opera one night, when she *personated Venus*. Her Car drawn by doves waited for her. She got into it, but not sit-ting steadily, as it ascended, she was thrown from *her Car*, when about 6 feet from the stage. Poor woman! She on her *back*. A *lamplighter* took Venus in his arms from the stage. She was not materially *hurt*, but very *much frightened*. The King and Queen were present. She was thought to be *but a secondary Singer*.

We must remember that Stevens wrote this memoir a good deal later, so he had probably read Burney, since he uses the same phrase "but a secondary singer".

On Monday, 31 May, again in *The Public Advertiser* we find:

> NEW MUSIC./ This Day is published, A Set of Duets for two Violins; composed / by Madam Sirmen. Price 7s.6d. / Printed for and sold by William Napier, at his Music / Shop, the Corner of Lancaster Court, Strand, near / Charing Cross . . . They were "Most humbly Dedicated to his Royal Highness the Duke of Glocester, by his Royal Highnesses devoted humble Servant Maddalena Laura Syrmen".

William Henry, Duke of Gloucester (1743–1805), was a younger brother of King George III and a great lover of Italy. He had been in Italy 1771–72, so he had possibly met Maddalena socially through his Italian contacts.

The last time we see Maddalena's name in *The Public Advertiser* is on Tuesday, 1 June 1773:

> NEW MUSIC
>
> *This Day is Published*
>
> Six lessons for the Harpsichord or Piano Forte, with Accompanyments of a violin and Violoncello, composed by Ernesto Eichner, Price 10s . . . A celebrated concerto performed by Madam Sirmen, composed by Sig. Cirri, 3s. 6d . . . Printed by Welcker, in Gerrard-street, Soho.

And

> HAY-MARKET. / For the Benefit of Signora SYRMEN / At the King's Theatre in the Hay-market / This Day will be performed the favourite Co/mic Opera call'd / La BUONA FIGLIUOLA, / The part of La Buona Figliuola by Signora Syrmen / (Being her last Appearance in that Character) / The Music by Signor Piccini. With Dances . . . Tickets to be had of Signora Syrmen, No. 3 in / Whitcomb Street, Leicester Fields.

Again, there is no mention of the singers; the chief attractions were obviously the dancers. *La Buona Figliuola*, or *La Cecchina, ossia la buona figliuola*, was first performed in England in 1766 after having had an enormous success in Italy. As Burney explains:

> In the year 1760, Piccini passing through Rome, in his way to Milan, was entreated to compose a comic opera for the *Teatro delle Dame* in that city, which had lately been very unfortunate. No *libretto* was ready, and application having been made to the poet Goldoni, at this time in Rome, he furnished the musical drama of *La Buona Figliuola*, from his comedy of *Pamela* in a few days.[20]

Stone says that Maddalena took part in performances at Mary-le-Bone Gardens during the summer of 1773, but I have found no factual evidence for this.[21] So, this was the end of Maddalena's career as a violinist and singer in London.

However, the fame of her compositions was obviously spreading. Her *Six Trios* were in the Hummel catalogue for 1771 and indeed were still there in 1802 and possibly as late as 1814. They had also been published by Sieber in Paris and Welcker in London in 1771. Her *Violin Concertos* had been published both by Hummel in 1772 and 1773 and in London by Napier in 1772 with Giordani's arrangement for keyboard also by Napier in 1773. Her *Violin Duets* were published by Hummel and Napier in 1773. Nevertheless, it is interesting to hear of a performance of one of her violin concertos in Stockholm.

The first Swedish string quartets were being written in the 1760s and 1770s by Anders Wesström (*c.* 1720–81), who had spent the four years from 1756 travelling in Germany and Italy with J.G. Naumann and had had violin lessons from Tartini in Padua. It was, of course, Naumann, another Tartini pupil, to whom Tartini had written to try to find a husband for Maddalena. In the Stockholm newspaper the *Dagligt Allehanda* for Sunday 23 October 1774 we read:

> Concertmaster Mr Ferling, in the Stora Ridderhus-salen at 4.30 pm complete (i.e. unabridged) vocal and instrumental music. Programme to include a Violin Concerto by Madame Syrmen played by Mr Ferling. Ticket price 6 Copper Daler.

Erik Ferling (1733–1808) was the first musician who had the courage to give public chamber music evenings in Stockholm. He appeared in performances between 1761 and 1789 as a violinist, conductor, concert arranger, and composer on around seventy occasions in Stockholm and on a few occasions also in Gothenburg. In 1790 he moved to Åbo (Turku) and became leader of the Musical Society, thus establishing an important link between the Finnish province and Stockholm.[22]

So this is how prints and manuscripts of Maddalena's music are still to be found in Sweden.

Notes

1. *Galpin Society Journal* II (11 March 1949), 27–31.
2. Osborn Collection, Beinecke Library, Yale University.
3. Potter, 211.
4. Potter, 213–14.

5. Potter, 215–16.
6. *History* IV, 672.
7. Potter, 218.
8. Potter, 219.
9. Potter, 220.
10. Potter, 222.
11. Potter, 223.
12. *History* IV, 504.
13. *History* IV, 498.
14. *History* IV, 500.
15. *History* IV, 499.
16. *Westminster Magazine* I (Jan. 1773), 69.
17. *Westminster Magazine* (1773), 69.
18. *General Evening Post* (London, 9–11 March 1773), 4. I am grateful to Patricia Howard for drawing my attention to this quotation.
19. Earl of Malmesbury, ed., *A Series of Letters of the First Earl of Malmesbury, His Family and Friends from 1745–1820* (London, 1870), I, 270.
20. *History* IV, 489–90.
21. *Stone*, 1656.
22. I am grateful to John Arthur Smith of Drammen, Norway, and Kerstin Schofield of Oxford for their help in finding this information.

Chapter 8

MORE TRAVELS

From now on, the glimpses we have of Maddalena's life become fewer. In November 1774, we find "The return of the violin virtuosa Signora Schirmen" to Turin, asking permission to give a concert on the 18th in the Teatro Carignano.[1] We have an amusing mention of the Teatro Carignano in Anna, Lady Miller, *Letters from Italy* (London, 1776); she actually toured in 1770–71:

> The theatre is under great restrictions from the police. Before an opera is to be performed, the King himself takes the pains to read it over, and to erase every line that can admit of an indecent or double meaning (although I believe the Serious opera is generally thought very decent). This attention is particularly paid to the theatre on account of the morals of the royal family. The king never goes to the Comic opera, nor permits any of his own family to go thither. The Princess of Carignan only frequents that theatre— also in regard to the dances, as the Italian taste is more inclined to the grotesque than the serious, the danseuses jump very high, and kick up their heels in a more surprising than graceful manner; but if their attitudes happen to become unguarded, they have a sharp reprimand from the police. The delicate Zamperini, after her return from England, expressed too much licentiousness in her action and manner, for which she had an immediate order from

> the Duchess of S—y, to quit at once those airs which La
> Signora instantly obeyed—The black drawers worn by the
> danseuses have a very disgusting appearance.[2]

Whether or not Maddalena's concert took place, we do not know.

In 1775 the financial state of the monarchy at Turin seems to have been rather precarious. In March the king ordered that a special opera performance should be staged in honour of the wedding of the future King Carlo Emanuele IV to Madam Clotilde of France the following September. The Cavalieri who managed the Teatro Carignano said there was no money available to stage something suitable for the occasion, so the Society gratefully accepted the loan of L20,000 from the City of Turin. The work chosen was *L'Aurora*, the music by Gaetano Pugnani to a libretto by Gian Domenico Boggio. Maddalena was suggested as second woman, but in the event does not seem to have been one of the performers. The performance was not a great success in spite of having Lucrezia Agujari in the cast. She was paid 600 zecchini compared with the castrato's 330 zecchini and the tenor's 120 zecchini, but the highest paid performer was the first dancer who was paid a handsome 800 zecchini.[3]

Maddalena was far from idle. Between 1775 and 1777, the first three of her violin concertos were published singly in Paris:

> CONCERTO / A / Violon Principal, / Premier & Second
> Violon, / Alto & Basse. / Hautbois et Cors ad libitum. /
> Composé a / Madame Syrmen / Oeuvre II / Prix 3^lt. 12^c / A
> Paris / Chez Borrelly rue et vis a vis la ferme de l'Abbaye
> St Victor / Et aux Adresses ordinaires / En province / Chez
> M^rs les M^ds de Musique.

The title pages of the second and third concertos are similar except that they end with "Grave par Mlle Hyver". Did Maddalena visit Paris to oversee their publication or were they pirated from the Hummel editions?

Advertisements for the Venier edition of Maddalena's *Six Duets for Two Violins* appeared both in the *Mercure de France* in April and in *Affiches, annonces, et avis divers* on 19 October 1775:

> SEI / DUETTI / Per due Violini. / Composti Dalla Sigra /
> MADDALENA LAURA / SYRMEN / Opera V^A. /
> Nuovamente Stampata a spese di G. B. Venier. / Prix 7#.
> 4f. Gravée par Richomme. / A PARIS. / Chez Mr Venier

Editeur de plusieurs Ouvrages de musique rue St Thomas du / Louvre vis-à-vis le Chateau d'eau, et aux adresses ordinaires / En Province chez tous le M^{ds} de musique. / A.P.D.R.

As far as we now know, the final composition of Maddalena's to be published was a *Violin Sonata in A major* from the Viennese publishers Artaria, with the plate number 94. Artaria started to publish music around 1776, and this sonata was Maddalena's only work to be published singly. The piece has a curious publishing history. First, it was edited by Tranquillo Mollo, later to be Joseph Haydn's editor. In 1793, Mollo left Artaria to open his own music publishing house. Although the title page and Artaria catalogues said that it was written by Lodovico Sirmen, records kept by the firm show that Maddalena was the real composer. Artaria continued to include the work in its catalogues up to 1786, at least.

Lodovico's career continued to be successful. In June 1778 and also in 1781, he wrote and directed the music for the S. Antonio celebrations at the church of S. Apollinare Nuovo in Ravenna. He was also paid to perform at many academies or private concerts. On 7 July 1780, in the theatre he played a violin concerto and sang some funny songs (*canto alcune arie buffe*) "but he was more skilful at playing with a ball than singing".[4] In the library of the Casa Goldoni in Venice there is a libretto:

> L'AMORE / ARTIGIANO / DRAMMA GIOCOSO / PER MUSICA / *Da rappresentarsi* / NEL NOBIL TEATRO / Di Ravenna / LA PRIMAVERA DELL'ANNO / MDCCLXXX / *Dedicato alle Nobilissime, e* / *Gentilissime* / DAME, E CAVALIERI. / In Ravenna per Antonio Roveri / *La Musica è del celebre Sig. Floriano Gassman* / Primo Violino, e Direttore dell'Orchestra il celebre Sig. Lodovico Sirmen di Ravenna.

The cast consisted of a *Primo Ballerino Serio* and *Prima Ballerina Seria*; four *Groteschi*, two men and two women; two *Terzi Ballerini*; and two *Quarti Ballerini*. One wonders if this was the occasion when Lodovico sang his funny songs.

In 1782 he became Violin Teacher at the *Collegio dei Nobili*, a post he held until 1794 or 1796. So, he was an important musician in his own region and played a significant part in the musical life of Ravenna, even performing as far away as Rimini and Lugo. In 1785 he was

playing joint first violin in the opera orchestra at Lugo for a performance of *Il matrimonio in commedia* by Luigi Caruso.[5]

We next hear of Maddalena in 1779 as a singer in Dresden. Until the
Seven Years' War (1756–63) Dresden had been one of the most
cultured capitals of Europe. Among the musicians who had been working there were Carl Friedrich Abel, Johann Hasse (1699–1783), who
had been *Maestro di Coro* at the Incurabili (1735–39) in Venice, and
his wife, the singer Faustina Bordoni. The city had been devasted in
1760, and most of the Italian musicians, including the Hasses, had been
dismissed. The Elector Friedrich Augustus III was himself a keyboard
player capable of playing from a full score. Gradually the economic
and cultural conditions started to improve, the Italian opera began
again but on a much smaller scale, and Antonio Bertoldi was appointed
Direttore di Piaceri, literally "Director of Entertainment", and it must
have been he who invited Maddalena to Dresden. But why should she
be invited? I think we can see Tartini's influence again. The composer
Johann Gottlieb Naumann was the Elector's Kapellmeister to whom
Tartini had written when trying to find a husband for Maddalena. She
would have known Abel well from her London days; he had also
worked in Dresden before the Seven Years' War. There were two other
Tartini pupils in the orchestra, Joseph Schuster (1748–1812) and Crist-
oforo Babbi (1745–1814), whom Maddalena had probably met at
Faenza.

Burney had dismissed Maddalena as being "but a secondary singer";
however, in her contract signed 1 September 1779 her salary was to be
1,700 thalers, whereas the next singer, Bondini, was only allowed 991
thalers. Maddalena's contract still has to be found, but Bondini's of the
same date reads:

> This contract will be held binding just as if it had been
> executed by a Notary. It affirms that Caterina Bondini has
> been hired into the service of His Highness, the Most
> Serene Elector of Saxony, for the period of one year with a
> salary of 350 Hungarian regali. For her part, Signora
> Bondini agrees to sing as she is directed in chamber music
> concerts as well as in the opera, both serious and comic.
> She agrees to accept willingly whatever parts Signor Bar-
> toldi gives her in his role of impressario for the opera com-
> pany, in those works which he produces for the pleasure of
> His Highness, the Most Serene Elector of Saxony. This
> contract goes into effect on September 1 of the current year

[1779] and obliges Signora Bondini to agree to an extension of her contract up to a period of five years, with the same stipulations and conditions. If this contract is not to be renewed, notice of such a determination is to be provided four months in advance of the end of the season. This contract is executed in good faith in two copies and signed on September 1, 1779 by . . . Antonio Bertoldi, Director of Entertainment, to His Majesty King Frederick August, Elector of Saxony and Caterina Bondini.[6]

We know little about Maddalena's time in Dresden. On 2 October 1780 Bertoldi advertised the new opera season which continued until March the following year. Among the operas to be performed were Cimarosa's *L'Italiana in Londra* and *L'Avara* by Pasquale Anfossi. Both these composers had worked as *maestro di coro* for the Venetian *Ospedale dei Derelitti*; Anfossi, 1773–77 and Cimarosa, 1782–84. Perhaps Maddalena travelled with the court and had her music performed in other places besides Dresden, since manuscript copies of her compositions are to be found in libraries in Berlin, Münster, Tübingen, and Weimar. Dresden had had strong ties with Russia for many years. As early as 1731, the court there had sent a troupe of Italian musicians to the Russian Imperial Court. In 1784, Maddalena was invited to Russia.

Now here we return to the manuscript of Gamba Ghiselli, obviously the gossip-column writer of Ravenna:

> After the rumour spread throughout the region that Madam Lombardini, the wife of Lodovico Sirmen, had died in Dresden, she apparently rose from the dead, for she wrote to her husband that she had been invited to "Moscovia" in the spring of 1783 to perform as *prima donna* in the Imperial Theatre of Petersburg for the substantial fee of 8 thousand scudi. She invited him to join her in Petersburg, and said she was in a position to guarantee that he would be offered a place as first violinist which would obviously be to his great advantage, and claimed that through her contacts she could obtain for him an even more prestigious place at the Imperial Chapel, attached to that of the sovereign. Everyone was curious to see whether Sirmen would accept his wife's proposal or refuse this advantageous offer due to his obligations towards Countess

Zerletti. She was opposed to this journey and had a lot of
influence on him.[7]

For how long Lodovico's liaison with the Countess Zerletti had been
going on, we do not know, but he and Maddalena cannot have spent
much time together for about thirteen years. No wonder the charming
Lodovico had been able to find someone to take Maddalena's place.
Seemingly, however, Maddalena had not completely forgotten her
husband. Ghiselli goes on to say that in any case, in spite of his affair
with the Countess Zerletti, Sirmen finally decided to join his wife; he
obviously hoped this would further his career. According to Ghiselli,
although he had his post at the *Collegio dei Nobili* he decided to leave
for Lapland [surely the name was a geographical mistake] on 2 April
1783, and from there he was going to travel to Russia with his wife.
Since he was planning to stay there for several months, he arranged to
rent out his houses in Ravenna. He owned two, one in which he lived
and another which he had recently bought.

Travelling conditions must have been difficult. An Englishman,
John Richard, wrote:

> I set out from St Petersburg in the month of October, which
> proved rainy and disagreeable, in a coach I purchased that
> had no seats, but a mattress or feather bed being spread on
> the bottom, it renders it very commodious for travelling. I
> engaged a carrier for twelve roubles, which is about two
> pounds ten shillings sterling, to drive me with three horses,
> which they usually do abreast, and which journey he per-
> formed in thirteen days; the distance is 488 English miles.
> . . . Winter is the best time for travelling, as the snow is
> froze, whereas in summer the roads are terrible.[8]

One hopes that the Sirmens—with Giuseppe Terzi—travelled more
luxuriously than John Richard on his way from St Petersburg to
Moscow.

Musicians from Venice were always welcome in Russia. Among the
well-known composers who had worked there were Galuppi, Traetta,
Paisiello, Cimarosa, Locatelli, and Sarti. In 1782 Catherine the Great's
son, Pavel Petrovich, and his wife, Maria Feodorovna, visited Venice
incognito as the *Conti del Nord* and were treated as royalty for nearly a
week.[9] The entertainments included a concert by eighty girls from the
four *ospedali*, and the accounts reveal payments to Cubli and Lucovich
from the Mendicanti. Antonia Cubli, like Maddalena, had been a pupil

of Tartini and was now *Priora*. Antonia Lucovich was a singer and soloist in the many oratorios performed at the Mendicanti. Guardi painted a picture of the concert, which is now in Munich in the Alte Pinakothek, where the girls playing instruments and singing can be clearly seen wearing their lace collars.

On the same grand tour the Russians visited Dresden, so Maddalena could well have met Pavel Petrovich and his wife there, or at least some of their entourage. We do not know the terms on which the Sirmens were tempted to go to Russia, but unfortunately for them, by the time they got there, Catherine the Great had decided to completely reorganize the cultural life of St Petersburg, putting it more in the hands of the Russians and trying to reduce the Italian influence. Some of the Italians left or were dismissed. Economies were made, salaries and contracts reviewed and only renewed if the artist had been successful and appreciated by the court and public. Artists arriving in Russia could be engaged if there was a vacancy but only after they had been auditioned; fortunately we know that Maddalena, at least, got some work.

In 1765 Catherine had opened a *Casa d'educazione* in Moscow to educate young Russian artists. She wrote to the chairman:

> A school is to be established under the supervision of the Committee Chairman in which both males and females will be able to pursue careers in the Russian theatrical, musical, and dance arts, as well as in the various essential theatrical crafts. The goal of such an institution must be not only to form artists capable of secondary roles, but those able to replace foreign artists with those of our own nationality.[10]

Concerts were organized at the *Casa d'educazione* by Ernest Wanzura on Fridays and Sundays during the period 25 February to 7 March 1784. Maddalena played at one of these on 18 February and according to the *Moskovskie Vedomosti* in February: "This celebrated violin virtuosa has drawn praise from all the major courts and cities of Europe for her phenomenal playing". She also played twice at the Petrovsky Theatre, run by the English impresario Michael Maddox, but seemingly as a singer and keyboard player. She performed in St Petersburg on 13 April and 7 May, two violin concertos of her own composition, and also sang on the same occasions. On 13 April the performance was for a so-called Gallery concert at court and on 7 May at the Kamenny Theatre. Presumably Maddalena and Lodovico gave

other concerts, and perhaps Lodovico found an orchestra to employ
him. Maddalena's departure from Russia was announced in the *Sankt
Peterburskie Vedomosti* on 27 September 1784. By coincidence, in
1784 an anonymously written violin tutor was published in St Petersburg called *Skrypichnaya shkola ili nastavlenie igrat'na skrypke*,
consisting of twenty-seven pages. A copy is to be found in USSR-Lsc
(shelfmark 15.5.3.74). It is probably the first violin method to have
been published in Russia, and it would be pleasurable to think that the
writer was inspired by Maddalena's playing.[11]

We hear nothing specifically about Lodovico in Russia. However,
by May 1784, he was already back in Ravenna, presumably to the
delight of himself and the Countess Zerletti, but finding family problems which demanded his attention. These problems concerned his
"figliastra" Alessandra. This means literally "stepdaughter", although
we always assume she was his and Maddalena's daughter; it is more
likely to be Gamba Ghiselli's mistake. Alessandra had been sent to the
convent of S. Cecilia in Faenza at the end of the year 1782. Ghiselli
goes on to say she was going to be educated there under the supervi-
sion of Sister Teresa Bertoni, a most distinguished lady who was Vice-
Prioress at that convent. In her father's absence, the girl had been taken
away from the convent on the initiative of the Countess Zerletti and
Alessandra was now living with her. In the evening of 10 July (1783),
the Countess Zerletti came back from Faenza in the company of
Sirmen's daughter. The reason Countess Zerletti took her away was
that the girl suffered from a kind of infection (stye?) which had
developed below an eye. She decided to entrust her to Bianchini (the
doctor at Ravenna) for treatment and chose not to take her back to the
convent until she had completely recovered.[12] When Sirmen came
back, he forced his daughter, who had long been perfectly healthy, to
return immediately to the convent in Faenza and into the care of Sister
Bertoni.

> The girl left in sobs and tears as she did not want to part
> from her beloved Countess Zerletti, with whom she had
> stayed all these months . . . The girl was very good looking,
> graceful and affectionate. The Countess allowed her all the
> entertainment that she had herself—it is thus hardly
> surprising that the girl did not want to go back to the
> Convent. She left for Faenza on 22 September 1784.[13]

Between 1785 and 1786 Lodovico was finally joined by his wife at Ravenna, but the situation was difficult because of Lodovico's friendship with Zerletti and the relationship of Maddalena with Don Terzi.

We really do have to admire Maddalena for her sheer energy. In 1785 she was back in Paris. During the years she had been away from there, Giovanni Battista Viotti (1753–1824) had, with the help of the new style violin bow, introduced by François Tourte in 1775, revolutionized violin playing. Her first concert was at the *Concert Spirituel* on 5 May, Ascension Day, 1785. The type of programme had not changed much over the last seventeen years. There were symphonies by Abel and Sterkel, and along with songs and a clarinet concerto by Soler, there were two violin concertos both written and performed by Mme Sirmen. The *Mercure de France* wrote on 7 May:

> Mme Sirmen, the woman violinist who was such a sensation when she first performed here 14 years ago, played again but the reaction was less favourable. She preserves those characteristics of the Tartini School—charming tonal quality, and a playing style that is full of grace and emotional intensity, especially since she is a woman—that are, perhaps, somewhat neglected nowadays. Her playing style, however, is just the same as it was when she appeared here 14 years ago and, is therefore, extremely out of date. For some time now, violinists have placed more importance on speed of playing instead of tonal quality and on feats of skill instead of in imitating the singing voice. Unfortunately Mme Sirmen may have been able then to astonish her listeners' ears, but she can do so no longer. While far from intending to criticise her artistry, the reviewer believes Mme Siremen would do well to change her playing style so that it conforms to what is fashionable today. If she does, then we do not doubt that she will again receive the same enthusiastic applause that she did heretofore.

On 15 and 26 May she played concertos by Viotti; this was probably a mistake since their technical brilliance could have been too difficult for her.

As far as we know, this was the end of Maddalena's international career as a performer. Did she willingly give it up, or was it the fact that the French Revolution, which was to shatter Europe, was on its way and the rumblings of discontent were already to be heard? But her music continued to be reprinted, so presumably played, but since these were the days before composers were paid royalties, she probably never knew how many copies had been sold. Maddalena must have been a very sad person when she went back to Ravenna; let us hope that the faithful Terzi was able to console her.

In November 1785, Maddalena took Alessandra to another convent at Ancona, probably to place a good distance between her and Zerletti:

> Signora Sirmen had left for Ancona already on the 15th of that November (1785). She left her daughter there in a convent and continued her journey to Naples. She then went to Ravenna to stay with her husband; but she was not going to stay long. He had wasted some money which she had sent him to invest profitably. But he had in fact failed to invest most of it and had squandered it on personal expenses. This caused his wife a lot of distress, she was very jealous of the Countess Zerletti and believed that the Countess was the reason why her husband did not accompany her on her journeys. However, despite this jealousy, when Zerletti came to Ravenna from the countryside, she stopped for lunch at Signora Sirmen's who did not have a house in Ravenna but lived in a cottage by the Cella Bridge which had been recently bought by her husband. Signora Sirmen in turn had lunch at Zerletti's house the Sunday after St Martin, though on that occasion they hardly respected the rules of decency and Sirmen went back to her cottage as soon as lunch was over. Signora Sirmen had a Venetian priest with her who always accompanied her on her journeys, ever since the first days of her marriage. This priest escorted her to Ravenna on this occasion too. During this stay he asked the Archbishop permission to celebrate Mass and was asked to show his certificate and documents. He could only show a certificate that he had celebrated Mass in December 1784. Since he showed no document which could prove that he had ever given Eucharist after that date, the Archbishop did not think it appropriate to do so on this occasion. As a result of this the priest left with Madam and appeared to be unimpressed with the Archbishop.[14]

Whoever thought that soap operas were a recent invention? The saga continues:

At this time (mid-October 1786) the famous Madam Sirmen came back to Ravenna. She came with that priest of
hers who kept accompanying her in all her journeys and
who had left Venice with her just after her wedding . . . she
went to see (Zerletti) on various occasions and she went
with her to S. Pietro in Trento and to visit the Countess
Angelica Ginanni, where they spent a number of evenings
in conversation. But despite all appearances, they were
hardly on good terms with each other. [15]

Among Jane Berdes' papers which are now at Duke University,
North Carolina, are to be found some photocopied pages of accounts
from an unnamed institution. These entries describe income from rents
from houses and land owned and for boarding fees for girls placed
within the convent. The fees are all paid six months in advance. The
photocopies are not complete, but we can read with interest that on 16
November 1785 Signora Laura Sirmen paid 15 scudi for Alessandra;
on 17 May 1786 Signor Lodovico paid the same amount, and the
following 17 November Signora Laura paid the 15 scudi. This is a very
early example, I would have thought, of a wife earning money, so she
pays her share of probably what amounted to school fees. She was
obviously a very independent-minded lady. The payments continue
until 17 November 1798. The following year Alessandra married
Francesco Leonardi.

Notes

1. *Bouquet* I, 368.
2. *Miller* I, 200.
3. *Bouquet*, I 369–70.
4. *Ghiselli* III, c.4.
5. Paolo Fabbri, "I teatri settecenteschi della romana estense: Lugo", *Romagna Arte e Storia*, II no. 8 (May-August 1983), 55–76.
6. Dresden Staatsarchiv Opera Ledgers 1779, Loc. 908 Schauspiele und Redouten auf dem Churfürst Kleinen Theatre Beit, vol. VII 1790 Blatte 54^{r}-^{v}.
7. *Ghiselli* VI, cc. 93^{v}–94^{r}.
8. John Richard, *A Tour from London to Petersburgh, and from Thence to Moscow* (Dublin, 1781), 47.

9. Elsie and Denis Arnold, "Russians in Venice: The Visit of the Conti del Nord in 1782", 123–30, in *Slavonic and Western Music: Essays for Gerald Abraham*, ed. M.H. Brown and E.J. Wiley (Ann Arbor and Oxford: UMI Research Press and Oxford University Press, 1985), 123–30.

10. Imperial Theatre Archives, II, 114.

11. I am grateful to Nigel Yandell for this information.

12. *Ghiselli* VII, cc.15^v–16^r

13. *Ghiselli* IX, c. 76.

14. *Ghiselli*, cc. 85^v–87^v.

15. *Ghiselli* XIII, cc. 6.

Chapter 9

FINAL YEARS

One of the many problems to be faced when writing about Maddalena is that the only surviving documents written by her are her wills—she wrote two and a codicil. The first is dated 9 June 1798, then followed a codicil on 30 April 1806, and the final will is dated 15 September 1817.[1] She died 15 May 1818. Here we again meet the businesswoman (a complete translation of her wills is included in appendix D). Both wills and codicil were written in Venice from her own house on the Fondamenta Nuove 3117.

In her first will she sounds extremely prosperous and is generous in leaving gifts of money to relatives and friends. She starts with Lodovico: "I leave as a one off payment to my husband a legacy of 200 ducats, namely 200 ducats" as though she is not going to leave him a penny more. "I wish the Rev. G. Terzi to have the use, during his life-time, of the house owned by me and situated in Venice on the Fondamenta Nuove", and "All the furniture, household linen and other domestic items to be found in my house I wish to pass on to the Rev. Terzi for his own use, without him needing to account for it to any person". She also leaves him ". . . the use during his lifetime of the sum of 2,000 ducats held by Francesco Pisani, with the exception of 150 ducats which I freely leave him, and of the 150 to be used, should the need arise, for my funeral expenses". She leaves a generous 500 ducats to her adopted daughter, Angela, who according to the will of 1817 had lived with her since about 1795. In all she seems to have had about 3,650 ducats to leave in cash plus a house in Venice and property in Ravenna. At a very rough count this was probably the equivalent of about £500, a goodly sum in those days. She must have left the Mendicanti with some money but, of course, her dowry went to her husband and probably the Mendicanti money was used to keep the household in its early days. She must have looked after the money she earned very carefully. After all, as we have seen, she even sent money to Lodovico to invest, but, alas, he squandered it on the Countess Zerletti. Maddalena was obviously a very able lady indeed.

Maddalena's wills are not quite the only documents in existence that she herself wrote. I quote from the catalogue of the London auction house of Christie for a sale to be held on 20 December 1972:

> Tartini (G): A Letter ... to Signora Maddalena Lombardini ... an important Lesson for Performers on the violin. Translated by Dr Burney. English and French title and text 10pp. 4to. unbound London 1771—loosely inserted are two short Ls. s. of Maddalena Laura Lombardini Syrmen, to her bankers Busoni, in Paris, 5.3.1808 and 16.3.1811, together 1½p.4to., with franked address covers—a newspaper cutting advertising Sig^{ra} Sirmen's Benefit concert at Almack's, 15.IV, 1771.

Alas, this lot was not sold in the sale. It was either withdrawn, or sold elsewhere at a later date. Their significance is that good business-woman that she was, she still had money in a bank account in Paris—perhaps in the event she did get some money from her music published there. One wonders where those letters are now!

Gaetano Ravaldini paraphrases Gamba Ghiselli's account of Lodo-vico's later life.[2] He says that again misfortune, this time of a political nature, shattered the calm life of Lodovico. He was a well-known unbeliever, and his name appeared in an anonymous satire in verse which was published in Ravenna in the summer of 1798 which listed him among the main local subversives. It said, "Of course, Sirmen was insane", and someone wrote in the margin, "a celebrated violinist, a fanatic anti-catholic, who by his own confession admitted that he had not come near the sacraments for 30 years". An unbeliever, in 1798 he signed his firm acceptance of the constitution and as a result of this in May 1799 he was arrested, along with Clemente Magni, while hiding in a cornfield next to his villa at S. Pietro in Vincoli, "not forgetting to take his favourite violin with him". Meanwhile his house in Ravenna was sacked by Croatian troops joined at Ravenna by the Austrian army. On 21 June the same year he was forced to make a public confession and had to go on foot to the Basilica of Classe for absolution after which he asked permission to retire to the Capucin convent. His confession was received by the parish priest of S. Clemente, Father Luigi Badessi, who was asked to do this by the Archbishop Codronchi. Lodovico was able to return to his profession, thanks to the stability of the new institution *filofrancesi* after the terrible events during the years around the end of the century. In 1806 he became one of the members (*prefetto*) of the committee called together to ensure the efficiency of the theatre orchestra.

Among the Berdes papers to be found in Duke University, North Carolina, there is a document concerning Don Giuseppe Terzi "Ex-gesuita e Nobili di Bergamo". This is a request made by Terzi and drawn up by notary dated 1805 that his pension of 120 ducats, formerly awarded him by the Republic of Venice and paid until 5 June 1802 under the Napoleonic regime in Venice, be continued. The reason it had stopped is given on the grounds that the priest is a native of Bergamo, now outside the jurisdiction of the *Territorio Imperiale* (Napoleonic regime). Instances are quoted of other ex-Jesuits who receive a pension and whose circumstances might give rise to doubt as to their eligibility. The outcome of the case is established by the Treasury, namely that G. Terzi's pension be reinstated. Unfortunately there is no reference as to where this document was found.

Maddalena's codicil, dated 30 April 1806, tells quite a different story from the will of 1798. The hundred ducats which previously had been left to her brother-in-law and to the poor of the district are now to be given to her servant Anna. She goes on to say ". . . in view of my changed circumstances, and since I am no longer in a position to offer benefits, and since I have no more than a few items of silver which I have retained from the past to serve me in case of need . . ." What had happened to her money? The obvious explanation is the occupation of Venice by the Austrians. In April 1797 Napoleon had secretly sold Venice to them, and in May Venice was invaded; almost no resistance was offered and so came the end of the Venetian Republic. As always, in times of war, the currency suffered, and this is probably the reason for Maddalena's newly found poverty. It is tragic to think that a famous composer, whose works were still in print, should suffer penury. It is not as if she had been forgotten; for example, three of her concertos were in the Hummel catalogue continuously from 1776 until 1819.

Lodovico died 18 January 1812. The best description we have of him was written after his death:

> Signor Lodovico Sirmen passed away yesterday due to an organic disease in the stomach. He has left no heirs, except for a daughter married to Signor Leonardi and living in Rimini. He was taken to his own chapel in the countryside where he was buried. He died aged seventy-three years of age and was still the strong man he had always been. He was a good violinist and composer; he had considerable success in the European capitals: Rome, Florence, Milan, Turin, Venice, and even Amsterdam, London, and Paris. He started life with no income. Due to his extreme success, however, and with the help of his wife Laura Lombardini, an excellent violinist herself, he managed to earn an annual income of over a thousand *scudi* and have the linen, furniture and valuables appropriate to a respectable man. He continued to display competence and ability in handling all sorts of mechanism till the very last days of his life. Mechanical objects had no mystery for him and all worked perfectly after they had passed through his hands. He made some excellent violins, some carillon clocks and many more things. He lived quietly, but was suspected of having joined the freemasons: many thus doubted his eternal life, especially as he died with a boldness which surpassed the just confidence of a good Christian. This suspicion is confirmed by the fact that some of his associates, among whom Signore Thomaso Lovatelli, who had been looking after him till his death, Signor Scala and Capitano Severi, formerly Lateran Canon, went to the site where he was buried and purified him from the stain left on him by the presence of a priest at his death although the priest had not given him extreme unction.[3]

Maddalena's final will is dated 15 September 1817. The paper on which it is written is interesting. At the top of each sheet is a stamp saying: "Su carta bollata da cent. 50". Still today in Italy, to write even a minor legal document you have to put a stamp on the paper—this must be a legacy of Napoleon. The text is rambling, especially regarding the ownership of land and houses, and it seems particularly strange to us nowadays that she had no performing rights or royalties from her music to bequeath; the possibilities of these came several decades after her death.

Her death certificate is to be found in the parish records of the church of SS.Giovanni e Paolo, Venice:

15 May 1818, Venice

> Signora Maddalena Laura daughter of the late Pietro Lombardini, and widow of the late Lodovico Syrmen, born in Venice, resident at Fondamenta nove no. 3117. Seventy-two years old after nine days of illness in bed [decubito] her life ended at 9 o'clock this morning. She will be buried tomorrow. She was visited by Dr Gaetano Ruggieri, licence 101, son of Gasperina Gambirasi.

We also find:

6 May 1818, Venice

> The Rev. Don. G. Terzi, son of the late Gottardo, and of Aurelia David, priest native of Venice, resident in our parish at Fondamente nove no. 3117, aged 82 years, after eleven days of pleurisy/pneumonia died at 3 am, certified by Dr Gaetano Ruggieri, licence 101.

How poignant it is that they died within nine days of each other.

Maddalena and Lodovico Sirmen's only child, Alessandra, was married to Francesco Leonardi of Rimini on 17 April 1790.[4] The dowry which Alessandra received from her parents was converted into additional property annexed to their home at Vergiano, just outside Rimini.[5] Francesco was active in Rimini's local government and served a term on the municipal council in 1797.[6] He died 10 November 1824. Alessandra and Francesco had six children; the third, Gregorio, by 1831 was a medical doctor. So as to pay for further studies in surgery in Paris, on 29 December 1834, Alessandra borrowed 200 scudi from two Rimini sources using her home in Vergiano as security.[7] Gregorio did not finish his study in Paris, but instead went to America and settled in New Orleans.

So ends the story of the life of this fascinating lady. Now, we must consider her music. We must remember that most of it was written when she was under thirty years old and one wonders why she stopped. Perhaps in her busy life there was little time for her to compose. She had to earn money, and her published music either brought in very little money, or none at all. So maybe she thought it was not worth the effort. Her violin concertos are very like the early Mozart ones, and again we have the thought that had she continued to compose, what direction would her music have taken?

Notes

1. VAS Notarile Serie 2, Pietro Occioni, 121.
2. Gaetano Ravaldini, "Appunti sulle origini della massoneria a Ravenna", *Rivista Massonica*, VIII (1976), 5, 8, 16–17.
3. Ravenna Biblioteca Classense, P. Raisi, Giornale, Mob. 3.2.M.2, VII, 28 January and 12 February 1812.
4. Rimini Archivio, Notaio F.A. Masi, 17 April 1790 records her dowry, as does Notaio L. Zumaglini 29–30 March 1813, Bol. XXX section I, f. 28 c. 374.
5. Rimini Archivio, Notaio L. Guerra, I, 20 February 1826, contains Francesco Leonardi's last will.
6. M.A. Zanotti, *Giornale di Rimini* (1797), 178; (1802), 218; (1816), 120.
7. Notaio L. Guerra, 29 December 1835, cc. 240^v.

Chapter 10

LIST OF COMPOSITIONS

by JANE BALDAUF-BERDES

Note: Not all the manuscript copies are complete, but I have been unable to check all the libraries cited. (E.A.)

Six String Quartets

Printed Editions

1769: SEI / QUARTETTI / A Violino 1, e 11, Viola, e Violoncello / *DEDICATI* / *Al Illustrissimo Signor Conte* / *BENEVENTO* / *Di San' Raffaelle* / E COMPOSTI DA / LODOVICO, E MADELENA LAURA SYRMEN / Prix 9# / Opera III / *A PARIS* / *Chez Madame Berault M^{de} Musique rue de la Comédie française Fauburg St Germain au Dieu de l'harmonie* / *Et aux adresses ordinaires* / *A.P.D.R.*

1773: *Six* / QUARTETTOS / *for two* / Violins / A / *Tenor and Bass* / Composed by / *Lodovico* and / Madelena Laura Syrmen / Price 10s.6. / *London*/ Printed for, & sold by Wm Napier, corner of Lancaster Court, Strand: / Where may be had by the above Author / Six Concertos for the Violin ... Pr. 1.1.0... D^o adapted for the Harp^d by Giordani. 1.1.0. / Also six Duets for two Violins 7s. 6d.

c. 1786: In the Sieber catalogue.

Prints: B–Bc Berault (V25.654); GB-Ckc Berault (RW.24.233.6.10), Lbl Berault (g.413 14a); US-Wc Berault (M452. S627. Op.3.Case).

Manuscripts: I–An (Ms.Mus. 28), Gi(1) (M.3b.24.23), Nc (Ms.22.3.8.), Bc (KK 126); GB-Cpl a fragment of Quartet no. 6 (Ms.81.no. 21).

Six Trios for Two Violins and Bass

Printed Editions

1769: Paris (?) Printed privately. Six / TRIOS / à / Deux VIOLINS et VIOLONCELLO obligé / *Dédiées* / *A Son Altesse Royale* / MADAME LA PRINCESSE / *D'Orange et de Nassau &c &c &c* / Composés / Par MADAME LOMBARDINI SIRMEN / *Eleve du célèbre Tartini de Padoue* / Oeuvre première.

1770: In Breitkopf catalogue

1771: In Hummel Catalogue: 'J.J. Hummel, Marchand au grand Magazin de Musique sur Vygendam, à Amsterdam'. Title page as above but continues with: *On peut les avoir a Amsterdam chez J.J. Hummel / Marchand & Imprimeur de Musique. Prix £3:10.*

1771: Six / TRIOS / à / *deux VIOLONS* / *ET* / VIOLONCELLO OBLIGÉ / Composés par / *Madame Lombardini Sirmen* / *Eleve du célèbre Tartini de Padoue* / Oeuvre Première Price 10.6. / LONDON / Printed by WELCKER in Gerrard Street, St Ann's Soho / Where may be had the greatest variety of New Music by the most celebrated Authors &c &c &c

1771: SIX / TRIO / A / Deux Violons et Basse / *Composés* / PAR / Mme Lombardini Sirmen / Eleve du celebre Tartini de Padoue / Oeuvre I^r / *Gravé par M^{dame} Sieber / Mis au jour par M^r sieber et compagnie successeurs de M^r huberty* / Prix 7# 4f. / A PARIS / *Chez L'editeur rue deux Ecus au pigeon blanc ou l'on trouve au / Grand Magazin de Musique Moderne Et aux adresses ordinaires / Mr Castraud Marchand libraire place de la Comédie a Lyon* / A.P.D.R.

Prints in GB–Lbl (g 471, Hirsch 111.376), Ckc (Rw 222–4/6); F–Pn (K 6070) and (K 6076); B–Bc (V.26.843) and (V. 7052); S-Skma; SF–TAa; US–Wc (M351.S65.Op.1.Case)

Manuscripts, some incomplete: D–Bds (5186–5190); S–L Saml. Kraus (386), Skma (W3–R), H (39); I–Bc (KK 126)

Modern Editions

Lauro Malusi (ed.), *Laura Maddalena Lombardini, Due Terzetti* (Padua 1983) from I–Bc (K K 126). These are nos. III and V from the Welcker ed.

Gloria Eive (ed.), *Trio a due Violini e Basso* in S. Glickman and M.F. Schleifer (eds.), *Women Composers, Music Through the Ages*, vol. 5 (New York: G.K. Hall & Co., 1998), 405–424.

Six Violin Concertos

Printed Editions

1772: A / CONCERTO / in / *SEVEN PARTS* / Composed by / MADELENA LAURA SYRMEN / *Opera III Price 3ˢ 6ᵈ* / N.B. *There will be One Concerto published Monthly, Till / the Six are compleated, composed by the same Author* / LONDON / *Printed for William Napier; the Corner of / Lancaster Court Strand.*

1772: TROIS CONCERTS / A / VIOLINO PRINCIPALE, / *Violino Primo & Secondo,* / *Alto & Basse.* / *Hautbois & Cornes de Chasse ad Libitum.* / *COMPOSÉES* / Par / *Madame* / M. L. SYRMEN / OEUVRE SECOND / *A AMSTERDAM chez J. J. HUMMEL,* / *Marchand & Imprimeur au Grand / Magazin de Musique.*

1772: as above but three concertos op. 3.

1772: op. 2 and 3 in Breitkopf catalogue

1773: *Six* / CONCERTOS / in / *NINE PARTS* / Composed by / MADELENA LAURA SYRMEN / *Opera III* / Price L1.1 / NB. These concertos being properly Adapted for the Harpsichord by Sigʳ GIORDANI, may be had separate Pʳ 7.6d. or may be play'd as Harpsichord Concertos by leaving out the Violin Principale. / *LONDON* Price L1.1. / Printed for Willᵐ Napier. Corner of Lancaster Court / Strand.

1775–7: CONCERTO / A / *Violon Principal,* Premier & Second Violon, / Alto & Basse.—*Hautbois et Cors ad libitum.* / COMPOSÉ PAR / MADAME SYRMEN / OEUVRE II / Prix 3ˡᵗ 12ᶜ / A PARIS / *Chez Borrelly rue et vis a vis la Ferme de l'Abbaye Sᵗ Victor / Et aux Adresses ordinaires / EN PROVINCE / Chez Mʳˢ le Mᵈˢ de Musique. / Gravé par Melle Hyiver.*

Complete prints in E–Mn, (M68–699/1) Napier edition

Manuscripts (some incomplete): B–Lc (fonds Terry 77–2, M–I); D
MÜu (M. 726); I–BC (KK 126), Gi (M.3b, 24, 25), TRa (N.
749/x.13.N.17), Vnm (Cod. It. IV. 1524 (= 11462), Nc (Ms 9651,
No. X. 1983), OS (Ms MUSICHE B. 2795); CS–Bb 89–D.A8)

Modern Editions

Jane L. Baldauf-Berdes (ed.), *Three Violin Concertos* (Madison: A–R
Editions, 1991). Concertos nos I, III, and V.

Six Concertos ... adapted for the harpsichord by Sig. Giordani

Printed Editions

1773: *Six* / CONCERTOS / *for the* / Harpsichord / *or* / *PIANO FORTE*
/ Composed by / MADELENA LAURA SYRMEN / *adapted for
the Harpsichord by* / Sig.ʳ Giordani. / Price Single 7s 6, with
Accompanyments £1.1s. / *London. Printed for Wᵐ Napier, Corner
of Lancaster Court* / *Strand, where may be had the above
Concertos for the Violin* / *price £1.1s and a Set of Quartettos by
Madam Syrmen for 10s.6d.*
1775–77? Longman & Broderip.
Prints in GB–Lbl Napier (R.M.17.c.4. (14)), Longman & Broderip (h.
73); I–Vc Napier; US–NYp Napier (*MYF 158620A); US–Wc
Napier (M1001.S64.Op.3.65.Case); also listed as M1011.S.98.
Case and M37.S.Case.
Manuscripts: D–WRz (Lb Mus IIIc.19)

Six Duets for Two Violins

Printed Editions

1773?: *SIX* / DUETTS / *for two* / Violins. / *Most humbly Dedicated to
his* / Royal Highness the Duke of / *GLOCESTER* / *by his Royal
Highnesses* / *devoted humble Servant*; / *Madelena Laura Syrmen* /
/ Pr. 7ˢ.6. / LONDON. / *Printed for and sold by William Napier at
his Music Shop* / the Corner of Lancaster Court, Strand. / *Where
may be had Composed by the above Author.* / VI Solo Concertos
for the violin £1.1s. Ditto adapted for the Harpsichord by Sigʳ.
Giordani £1.1s. The Harpsichord part of Ditto Single 7s. 6. VI
Quartetts 10s 6.

1775: SEI / DUETTI / Per due Violini / *Composti Dalla Sig^{ra}* / MADALENA LAURA / SYRMEN / *OPERA* V / *Nuovamente Stampata a Spese di G. B. Venier.* / Prix 7^# 4^f / *Gravée par Richomme* / A PARIS. / *Chez Mr Venier Editeur de plusieurs Ouvrages de musique rue St Thomas du* / *Louvre vis-à-vis le Chateau d'eau, et aux adresses ordinaires.* / *En Province chez tous les M^{ds} de musique.* / A.P.D.R.

1776: SIX SONATES / A / DEUX VIOLONS / Composées / *Par* / *Madame* / M. L. Sirmen. / *Oeuvre Quatriem.* / *A La Haye* / chez B. Humel. / *Prix f3.*

Prints in GB–Lbl (g 42^r. (12), g. 421.s (7), h.2910 (5)

Manuscripts: I–Gi (1) (N. 1.6.6.Sc.17), Ria (Ms 824), OS (Mss. Musiche B. 2796), Rc (Mss 6093–8), Mc (A.27.18.4)

Modern Editions

Cora Cooper and Karen Clarke (eds), *Six Duettos for Two Violins* (Bryn Mawr: Hildegard Publishing Co., 1994).

Attrib. L. Sirmen

1785: SONATA / *per il* / *VIOLINO E BASSO* / del / SIG^R. L. SIRMEN / *In Vienna presso Artaria Comp* / C.P.S.C.M. 94 40 Xuv.

Prints in D–Tu (Mk 90 S 5); I–Vc (Mus. No. 95); US–Wc (M287.A2 S4.Case).

Chapter 11

THE MUSIC

by

JANE BALDAUF-BERDES AND ELSIE ARNOLD

Maddalena Lombardini Sirmen was, as far as we know at the present time, the first woman to write string quartets, and very lovely they are too. Like everything she wrote, the music has to be heard, and heard played well: it is difficult to imagine its beauty by just looking at the parts on paper. She was not an innovative composer; the forms she used are simple.

Unfortunately, not many of Maddalena's compositions have survived. We have printed editions of the *Six String Quartets*, *Six String Trios*, *Six Violin Duets*, *Six Concertos for Violin*, a *Violin Sonata in A*, and a *String Trio in B flat*. There are anonymous manuscripts from the *ospedali* in the collections of the Conservatorio di Musica Benedetto Marcello in Venice and the library of the University of California at Berkeley; some of Maddalena's music could possibly be found there but it is difficult to identify since we have no known autographs. Manuscript copies of her printed music are found widely throughout Europe, and even in the United States of America a manuscript of the first *Duet for two Violins* is to be found in the Weiss Collection in the library of the Moravian Music Foundation at Winston-Salem, North Carolina.[1] Johann Friederich Frueauft, the

Moravian musician and composer, wrote in his diary on 3 January 1789 that he had obtained violin concertos by her for the Northern Province of the Moravian Church in America.[2]

It is interesting to track down why music, both in prints and manuscripts, has arrived in some of the libraries where it is to be found. For example, there is a badly damaged manuscript of the first *Violin Concerto in B flat* in Münster University Library. Originally it was in a collection owned by the Duke of Mecklenburg-Strelitz. He was the brother of Queen Charlotte of England and could very well have visited England and heard Maddalena play. This manuscript has a minuet finale which was replaced by a rondo allegro before it was published in 1772 and is scored for two flutes instead of oboes. Three German libraries hold material from the former Prussian State Library founded by Frederick the Great: the German State Library, Berlin, the West Germany Library, Marburg, and the University Library, Tübingen. Maddalena's music there could have been acquired when she was working in Dresden. The only complete printed copy of the *Six Violin Concertos* is to be found in Spain in the Biblioteca Nacional, Madrid. So, we find two second-generation Tartini violinist-composers working there during the last quarter of the eighteenth century. Filippo Manfredi (1729–80) and Gaetano Brunetti (1754–98) had both studied with Tartini's pupil, Nardini. The King, Carlos V, was a keen violinist and played second violin under Brunetti in royal ensembles.

Regarding Sweden, we have already heard of the performance of one of Maddalena's violin concertos by Erik Ferling in Stockholm on Sunday, 23 October 1774. He moved to Åbo (Turku), now in Finland, where there is a print of the *Trios*, and another copy of them is to be found in the former collection of the Akademiska Kapellet (University Orchestra) in Lund. Naumann, the Tartini pupil who tried to find a husband for Maddalena, also worked in Sweden from about 1777. The copies in Italian collections could easily have found their way there via more Tartini pupils or by professional musicians who had heard her music in Venice and other towns where concerts took place.

Maddalena's most important teacher of composition was undoubtedly Tartini. Ferdinando Bertoni, her teacher at the Mendicanti, was primarily a composer of operas for the theatre and religious vocal music for St Mark's and the Mendicanti. If Maddalena ever wrote any vocal music it has been lost. Her compositions are all for strings; after all, she was a violinist. Tartini's main teaching tool was his *Regole per arrivare a saper ben suonar il Violino* (Rules to understand how to play the violin).[3] Maddalena would have studied the music of Corelli, who was much admired by Tartini; in fact in Tartini's letter to her he suggests she should practise one of Corelli's allegros every day. She would have examined Tartini's own compositions—concertos, sonatas, and trio sonatas and would also have been in contact with the compositions of his other students.

Six String Quartets

(1) E flat Major, (2) B flat Major, (3) G Minor, (4) B flat Major, (5) F Minor, (6) E Major.

Like all musical forms, the string quartet—for two violins, viola and 'cello—evolved gradually. Four-part pieces for strings were found during the early part of the eighteenth century, but these were more like orchestral than chamber music and frequently there was a part for a keyboard instrument. In fact, Haydn's earliest so-called quartets could be played by a small orchestra. According to Giovanni Giuseppe Cambini the first public performance of a string quartet was arranged by Boccherini in Milan in 1765; the players were Pietro Nardini and Filippo Manfredi, violinists, Cambini, viola, with Luigi Boccherini playing the 'cello. Maddalena's quartets, however, are written in the normal late-eighteenth-century way of two violins, viola, and 'cello. Occasionally they have more interesting lower parts than those of Haydn's Op. 9 which were those advertised in the Berault catalogue of 1769, just below those of Maddalena. The form of Maddalena's quartets is uncomplicated: two movements, generally in a simple binary, ternary, or rondo form. The first movements are fairly conventionally written but in the second movements, Maddalena, like Haydn in his minuets, is inspired to experiment with sonorities and form: note the delicious texture she conjures up in the second half of the second movement of the first quartet, or the subtle reversal of major and minor modes in the third quartet's finale, the fiery virtuosity in the trio of the fourth, and the witty sparkling writing in the finales of the second and sixth. Perhaps the most arresting of all is the opening largo to the fifth quartet which could have been written by Mozart. The notes of these quartets are not difficult, but like the quartets of Mozart, it is far from easy to play them well, but very rewarding when performed by an accomplished string quartet.

QUARTET No. 5 FIRST MOVEMENT

Organizational Charts, by Jane Baldauf-Berdes

Six String Quartets

	1st Mov.	2nd Mov.
Quartet no. 1 in E flat major		
Keys	I-V; V-vi-I	[I] I–V; V–vi–I
Tempo	Andante ma con un poco molto	Allegretto
Meter	2/4	3/4
Form	Incipient ternary	Incipient ternary
Themes	5	5
Quartet no. 2 in B flat major		
Keys	I-V; V–vi–I	[I] I–V; V–vi–I
Tempo	Andantino	Allegro
Meter	2/4	2/4
Form	Incipient ternary	Incipient ternary
Themes	5	5
Quartet no. 3 in G minor		
Keys	i–III; III–i	[I] I–V–I/i–V–I
Tempo	Giusto	Allegro
Meter	4/4	2/2
Form	Incipient ternary	Rondo with 3 episodes
Themes	5	1
Quartet no. 4 in B flat major		
Keys	I–V–V–vi–I	[I] I–V–I
Tempo	Cantabile	Menuetto
Meter	4/4	3/4
Form	Incipient ternary	Minuet
Themes	5	
Quartet no. 5 in F minor		
Keys	i–V; V–I	[I] I–V; V–I
Tempo	Largo-Allegro	Minuetto/Allegretto
Meter	2/2	3/4
Form	Incipient ternary	Minuet and Trio
Themes	5	
Quartet no. 6 in E major		
Keys	I–IV-VI; V–III–i– V–I	[I] I–V; V–I
Tempo	Andantino	Con brio
Meter	3/4	2/4
Form	Incipient ternary	Rondeau
Themes	5	

Another complication, which applies to all Maddalena's publications, is that they are frequently so inaccurate. Did she ever have the opportunity to proof-read them, one wonders? When looking at the instrumental parts of the Bérault edition of the *String Quartets* in the British Library,[4] one has the feeling that they were not even part of the same edition, with conflicting expression marks and the occasional, impossible chord.

Six Trios or Sonatas for Two Violins and Bass

Trio no. 1 in F major	1st Mov.	2nd Mov.
Keys	I–V; V–vi–I	I–V–ii–vi–I
Tempo	Giusto	Allegretto-Menuetto
Meter	4/4	6/8. 3/4
Form	Incipient ternary	Rondo
Themes	5	1

Trio no. 2 in C major		
Keys	I–V; V–vi–I	[I] I–V–I
Tempo	Vivace	Menuetto Smorfioso
Meter	2/2	3/4
Form	Binary	Minuet & Trio
Themes	3	2

Trio no. 3 in D major	1st Mov.	2nd Mov.	3rd Mov.
Keys	I–V; V–I	[I, IV] I–V–I; IV-V–I	[V] I–V–I
Tempo	Allegro cantabile	Menuetto grazioso	Allegro assai
Meter [4/4]	4/4	3/4	2/3
Form	Rounded binary	Rounded binary	Rondo with 2 episodes
Themes	5	2	2

Trio no. 4 in A major		
Keys	I–IV–V	V–I
Tempo	Andante	Allegretto Smorfioso
Meter	3/4	2/4
Form	Rounded binary	Rondo with 3 episodes
Themes	5	1

Trio no. 5 in G major

Keys	I–V–IV–I; V–III–i–I	[I] I–V–I–III–vi–I
Tempo	Allegro moderato	Rondo Allegro
		Menuetto Allegro
Meter	2/4	2/2–3/4
Form	Incipient ternary	Rondo with 3 episodes
Themes	5	1

Trio no. 6 in F minor

Keys	i–III; III–vi–III	[I,i] I–V–vi–III–i/I
Tempo	Lento	Menuetto Allegretto
Meter	4/4	3/4
Form	Incipient ternary	Rondo
Themes	5	2

Maddalena's *Six Trios* were first published privately, possibly in Paris in 1769, and reprinted by Hummel in Amsterdam in 1770–71. Lodovico also published *Six Trios* with Hummel in Amsterdam in 1769, and some scholars have wondered whether Maddalena in fact wrote both sets. The title on the frontispiece of Maddalena's is "Six Trios", but they are then called "Sonatas" in the instrumental parts. Sonata II opens "Vivace" followed by "Menuetto Smorfioso" and "Trio". The dictionary translations of "smorfioso" are: "mawkish", "prissy", or "affected".

Trio in B flat for Two Violins and Bass

The manuscript of this trio formerly belonged to Dr Caffagni of Modena, who very kindly gave it to Jane Baldauf-Berdes, so it is now in the Special Collections Library of Duke University, North Carolina. He wrote to Jane:

> During the winter of 1974 I was approached by an antiques dealer who showed me a large box of books and manuscripts that the Bagnese family wished to dispose of. Among the manuscripts I found the one by Maddalena Lombardini Sirmen. There are many reasons to think that many of the manuscripts I examined during that evening of 1974 came from the Tacoli family, a very old and noble

family of Modena. Presumably a young Tacoli lady, who
married a Bagnese, took manuscripts and books with her.

Written on the title page of each part is: "*ad uso de Carlo Ferrari*" (for
the use of Carlo Ferrari). This could very well have been the brother of
Domenico Ferrari (1722–80), who was said to have been one of
Tartini's finest pupils. Carlo (*c.*1710–*c.*80) was a famous cello
virtuouso and composer of instrumental works. There are three movements: Allegro—Adagio—Allegro. This trio has been published as
"Maddalena Lombardini Sirmen" by Elsie Arnold and Gloria Eive in S.
Glickman and M.F. Schleifer (eds.), *Women Composers, Music
through the Ages* (New York: G.K. Hall and Co., 1998), 388–424.

Six Duets for Two Violins

Duet no. 1 in E flat major	1st Mov.	2nd Mov.
Keys	I–V; V–ii–V–I	I–V–I
Tempo	Allegro moderato	Menuetto
Meter	4/4	3/4
Form	Rounded binary sonata	Rounded binary sonata
Themes	5	4
Duet no. 2 in D major		
Keys	I–V; V–vi–I	I–V–I
Tempo	Larghetto	Allegretto-Menuetto
Meter	3/4	2/4
Form	Rounded binary sonata	Double period
Themes	3	2
Duet no. 3 in B flat major		
Keys	I–V; V–vi–I	I–IV–V–vi–I
Tempo	Allegro	Minuet-Trio
Meter	4/4	3/4
Form	Incipient ternary sonata	Minuet & Trio
Themes	5	2
Duet no. 4 in E major		
Keys	I–V; V–vi–I	I–V; V–VI/vi–I
Tempo	Allegro	Menuetto
Meter	4/4	3/4
Form	Incipient ternary sonata	Minuet
Themes	5	1
Duet no. 5 in A major		
Keys	I–V; V–vi–I	I–V; V–III–I
Tempo	Andantino	Allegretto
Meter	3/4	6/8
Form	Rounded binary sonata	a–á–a, variation, coda
Themes	4	

Duet no. 6 in C major

Keys	I–V; V–I	I–V–vi–V–I
Tempo	Allegro	Allegro brillante
Meter	4/4	2/4
Form	Ternary sonata	Theme/variations
Themes	6	A/Á/A/Á/A/Á/A

The duets could have been composed for teaching purposes at the Mendicanti, or even for husband and wife to play together. On paper they do not seem very interesting but when played by two really good violinists they are excellent examples of this genre.

Sonata in A major for Violin and Bass

As we have seen earlier, this Sonata was attributed to Lodovico but its publishing history shows it is by Maddalena. It seems far more virtuosic than her previous music, but, of course, she would have been considerably older when she composed it.

	1st Movt.	2nd Movt.	3rd Movt.
Keys	I–V; V–vi–I	[V] I–V; V–I	[I] I–V; V–vi–I
Tempo	Moderato	Adagio cantabile	Lento-Menuett
Meter	2/4	2/2	3/4
Form	Rounded binary	Arch	Rounded binary
Expression	Virtuosic	Short trans to	(a) Polonaise (b) sarabande (c) syncopation (d) minuet and march-like dotted motif present a parade of mixed moods

Notes

1. Jane Baldauf-Berdes wished to record her thanks to Rebecca Jenkins, New Carrollton, Md., and Dr James Boeringer of the Moravian Music Foundation for their help in drawing her attention to these documents.
2. Moravian Archive, Bethlehem, Pa., *Journal of Johann Friederich Frueauft, Jr., 1788–90.*
3. Venice, Museu Civico Correr ms 323.
4. g 413. (14a).

Chapter 12

THE VIOLIN CONCERTOS

by
JANE BALDAUF-BERDES

[This is extracted from Jane Baldauf-Berdes' master's thesis, "The Opp. 2 and 3 Violin Concertos by Maddalena Laura Lombardini-Sirmen (c.1735–c.1799)", submitted to the University of Maryland in 1979.]

Lombardini Sirmen belongs to that generation of composers who experimented with new forms of instrumental music and whose violin concertos bridged the span from such baroque and pre-classical composers as Vivaldi, J.S. Bach, and Giuseppe Tartini, to the classical masters: Haydn, Mozart, and Beethoven. Members of her generation include J.C. Bach, Haydn, Giovanni Giornovichi, Gaetano Pugnani, C.D. von Dittersdorf, Pietro Nardini, Luigi Boccherini, Tommaso Giordani, J.G. Lang, Antonio Lolli, and Josef Myslivecek, all of whom wrote violin concertos. Nardini and Lombardini Sirmen, as violin virtuosi, are among the best-known representatives of Tartini's celebrated performance method. Nardini alone, however, is the accepted standard bearer of the post-Tartini generation. Characteristics of

Tartini's compositional style are identified by Boyden in his *History of the Violin*, by Dounias in his study of Tartini's concertos, and by Duckles, Elmer, and Petrobelli, in their work on Tartini's Paduan School. These characteristics are: three movements, frequently in the same key; homophonic, rather than contrapuntal textures; long melodic lines including leaps of three octaves; technically demanding and complex ornamentation; and expressivity. Contributions to form either by Tartini in his 130-odd violin concertos or by acknowledged students are limited, for the most part, to the addition of tutti ritornellos to solo sonatas, the technique used by the young Mozart in his first seven concertos, the only ones he wrote for the violin.

Eighteenth-century transitional composers, including Lombardini Sirmen, built on the work of their mentors, in the best Enlightenment fashion, by experimenting with the concept of unity and variety in the one musical form that in itself serves as an analogy for the concept: the concerto.

> This individual character was to be expressed through a variety of rhythms, figures, and themes following one another in rapid alternation—continuing the kaleidoscopic tendencies of Pergolesi and Tartini. As variety increased, however, so did the need for larger, stronger forms that could gather up the more varied rhythms and themes into a broad but still compelling unity. Composers found their way towards these forms through a clarification and refinement of the sense of key: they brought the kind of tonal order built of triads to a peak of efficiency.[1]

Lombardini Sirmen Style Traits

It would be foolhardy to try to make a case for Lombardini Sirmen's six violin concertos as being either the best concertos written in their day or even among the best. Nonetheless, it can be stated that these concertos helped prepare the way for the best concertos composed in the Classic period. Supporting this statement abundantly are many progressive procedures in Lombardini Sirmen's compositional style, such as the consistency of her three-movement, fast-slow-fast overall design: her demonstration of embellishment technique based on Tartini's methods in slow movements; her use of different rondo forms in her third movements; her ability to control large tonal plateaux; and the appearance of well-delineated cadenzas, frequent chromaticism, notational innovations, inventive harmonies including major-minor alternation, and harmonic progressions ranging from secondary dominant to seventh chords in the cycle of fifths.

Instrumentation: Lombardini Sirmen's ensemble is the one Donald Tovey calls the "little old orchestra".[2] The commonly used instrumentation for the time was strings, oboes or flutes, and *corno di caccia*. Her orchestral colour, for the most part, is a blend of a melodic group of instruments—violins, including the solo violin, and oboes—and an harmonic group made up of the bass (cello) and the continuo, violas doubling the bass (except in rare instances where they are given a melodic or contrapuntal function), and horns reinforcing the harmony and providing punctuation. This typical eighteenth-century grouping would have been altered and enlarged in performances where possible, for example, by the addition of bassoons, perhaps, in Turin and Paris, played by members of the Besozzi family. This ensemble exceeds those used for Haydn's Concertos. Unlike Giornovichi, who wrote mainly *ad libitum* parts for oboes and horns in his orchestral tuttis, Lombardini Sirmen uses oboes to double first violins generally. Horns are similarly indispensable at times because they are the only source for middle harmonies, as, for instance, in cadenza preparation points.

Ritornello sections are frequently contrasted with the thin texture of three-part writing of solo sections in all three movements. This is especially pronounced in middle movements where in Concertos 1, 2, 3, and 6, ritornellos consist of mere opening and closing sections. In the middle movement of Concerto 4, there is an opening but no closing tutti; in that of Concerto 5, there is no tutti at all. This absence of a bass as the solo violin is accompanied by the first and second violins only, which is characteristic of some of Lombardini Sirmen's solo sections, results in a boldness of textural contrast that appears in works by such older generation Italian composers as Vivaldi and Tartini. It is characteristic too, of such post-Tartini composers as Giornovichi and Lolli. The high degree of technical competence demanded of the solo violinist in these concertos marks their composer as a true descendant of Tartini, the originator of the ornamental tradition that led to new levels of violin virtuosity. Domenico Ferrari, also a Tartini pupil, travelling virtuoso, and composer of instrumental sonatas, was among the first to *indicate* the use of harmonics, but the manuscript of the composer's Concerto no. 3, which he may have owned, calls for the highest register short of harmonics on the newer violin and would have called for harmonics definitely on the older instrument. Such individual treatment for instruments extends to tutti violins, which are never in unison, and to horns (in B^b, C, and F or E sharp) as well. Except for a few contrapuntal exchanges between strings at cadential points, textures in all the concertos are homophonic, as is typical of works composed by Tartini's descendants.

Allegro Movements: The principal violin follows the standard practice of the time in playing along with the orchestral tutti. Oboes climb high, even to the top of their range, d'''. In Concerto no. 1, where both horns and oboes have high notes, oboes also play almost constantly for 27 bars in thirds and sixths. Such demands on performers lessen in later concertos, suggesting either a stylistic simplification by the composer, a loss of the highly skilled oboists for whom she wrote originally, or an inaccurate chronology for the published works. The fact that one type of texture prevails throughout a section, generally, thus polarizing sonorities into large tutti or solo blocks of uniform sound, demonstrates that Lombardini Sirmen's style is not without its regressive traits. The accompaniment in solo sections is by violins only, omitting even basso and eliminating the need for figuration which appears elsewhere. The rewriting of the first and second violins, required by this realignment of roles if a three-part harmony is to be preserved, has first violins following the melody in thirds and the second violins acting as a composite of bass and viola parts.

Slow Movements: A pronounced feature of all the concertos is that, except for Concertos 4 and 5, middle movements are played mostly by the solo violin accompanied by upper strings. Brief opening and closing sections are performed as tuttis, with violas and basso joining in.

Rondo Movements: The finales show a continuous alternation of tutti and solo textures that does not occur in other movements. Variety of textures increases as new instrumental settings are given to each repetition of theme. While tutti writing for strings only does occur, there are also examples of short tutti-solo dialogue, lacking elsewhere in Lombardini Sirmen's instrumentation.

EXAMPLE 1: CONCERTO IN B FLAT MAJOR

EXAMPLE 2: CONCERTO 1 – KEYBOARD ARRANGEMENT

Form: During the 1760s the solo violin concerto responded to the changing conventions of the classical style. This response on the part of concerto composers involved the gradual absorption of sonata, three-part structure, and thematic and simpler harmonic contrasts into the standard tutti-solo alternating forms. As Crocker has observed, the compositional trend in the second half of the eighteenth century was toward larger, stronger, unifying forms in which composers would exercise their stylistic individuality. This observation holds true for Lombardini Sirmen's concerto writing methods.

As we have seen, a keyboard version of the concertos was made by Tommaso Giordani and published in 1773. It is interesting to compare the two versions:

The concertos reflect the three-movement (fast-slow-faster) plan, with concerto-sonata allegro first movements and rondo finales. The following chart illustrates Lombardini Sirmen's formal plan, including details of key, tempo, and meter, for the 18 movements in her six concertos:

Concerto No. 1	1st Movt.	2nd Movt.	3rd Movt.
Key	B flat major	F	B flat
Tempo	Allegro	Andante	Allegretto
Meter	4/4	3/8	2/4
Form	Concerto-sonata	Rounded-binary	Rondo
Concerto No. 2			
Key	E major	A	E
Tempo	Allegro	Andantino	Allegro non tanto
Meter	4/4	3/4	2/4
Form	Concerto-sonata	Rounded-binary	Rondo
Concerto No. 3			
Key	A major	A minor	A
Tempo	Allegro	Adagio	Allegretto
Meter	4/4	2/4	2/4
Form	Concerto-sonata	Rounded-binary	Rondo
Concerto No. 4			
Key	C major	G	C
Tempo	Allegro	Andante	Allegretto
Meter	4/4	3/4	6/8–3/4
Form	Concerto-sonata	Rounded-binary	Rondo with two minuet couplets

Concerto No. 5

Key	B flat major	E flat	B flat
Tempo	Maestoso	Adagio/Andante	no designation
Meter	4/4	2/4	3/4
Form	Concerto-sonata	Rounded-binary	Rondo

Concerto No. 6

Key	C major	A minor	C
Tempo	Allegro	Largo	Allegretto
Meter	4/4	4/4	3/4
Form	Concerto-sonata	Rounded-binary	Rondo

The general trend during the transition from the galant to the mature classical style of concerto writing was toward experimentation with ritornello-sonata form, and the first movements tended to increase in size dramatically. The following chart shows the range and proportion of the three movements of each of Lombardini Sirmen's known concertos through the number of measures (bars) in each movement:

Movement	No. 1	2	3	4	5	6
I	155	168	172	173	197	173
II	66	73	48	58	49	39
III	142	135	117	172	185	171

It will be noted that the opening movements grow by 42 bars or over 20%; slow movements shrink in an irregular but no less clear pattern of corresponding change; and finales, like first movements, grow. What is highly significant about the concertos as a set is that all six have first movements that are larger in terms of numbers of measures than the closing movements, suggesting that their composer focused on the new concerto-sonata form. In Concerto 1 for instance, the number of bars in the opening movement is 155 compared to 142 in the finale, giving a 44.5%–39% dominance to the first movement. The ratios prevail throughout the set, except for Concertos nos. 4 and 6, which are nearly identical in numbers of measures.

While the ritornello structure is the applicable form for all movements, the tutti-solo relationship is less that of equal participation in a dialogue than that of a master of ceremonies introducing a celebrity. Syntactically, Lombardini Sirmen's four-plus-four phrases that pause in half, and full cadences like clockwork take her search for form into the extremes of formalism.

The principle of unity and variety controls the high classic arrangement of the three movements: a concerto-sonata first movement, a slow, through—composed aria-like middle movement with a rounded-binary tonal structure—and a rondo finale. Signs of energetic experimentation with formal principles range from the use of an introductory theme as a unifying device to a set of six finales, none of which resembles the other.

First Movements: The first movement concerto plan used by Tartini was a five tutti, four solo structure. The standard plan by the 1760s was the four tutti, three solo design used by Lang, Giornovichi, and Carl and Anton Stamitz. Lombardini Sirmen's first movement sonata-concerto structure is invariably the three tutti, two solo one in which the first tutti either modulates briefly to the dominant (as in Concertos nos. 1 and 2) before returning to the tonic, or remains in the tonic after which the solo exposition effects the move to the dominant. The second or central tutti opens the development in every case and remains in the dominant throughout. In two instances—Concertos nos, 1 and 6, thematic material introduced by the solo exposition in the dominant returns in the recapitulation in the tonic key. Additional tonal contrast is provided by the second solo section which continues the development and carries the brunt of the recapitulation. In the latter three concertos' opening movements, the tutti section has a small share in the restatement of thematic material before being interrupted by the cadenza. Overall, the tutti proportion of the first movement's action is less than 40%, putting Lombardini Sirmen among those concerto composers who helped bring about the evolution of the modern concerto.

The first movements blend sonata form with concerto ritornello structure in the sense that there are three distinctive sections: exposition, development, and recapitulation superimposed on the tutti solo alternation, with the tonic return of the recapitulation coinciding with the restatement of expositional subjects. They cannot be defined as sonata form, however, in the ex-post facto sense of nineteenth-century understandings of the term. Opening tuttis usually present three or four distinct subjects—principal, secondary, and closing—and transitional themes. Concerto 4 is the exception in that its subjects are made up of ten different motives. Lombardini Sirmen's second themes are in the dominant in Concertos nos. 1 and 2, with the third subject re-establishing the tonic. Her solo sections modulate to the dominant, usually after having stated the full main subject in the tonic. Central tutti sections are smaller by about half on the average than opening tuttis. The proportion of the first and second tuttis is 34.8 bars to 18.8. Second tutti sections use subjects from the tutti exposition.

Slow Movements: As Andante, Adagio, and Largo movements set between two faster movements, Lombardini Sirmen's middle movements, since they are in slow tempo, could be said more or less to equal the first and last movements in time consumed in their performance. Unlike the faster movements, however, the middle movements are not easily analysed for their formal design. All six do have a binary construction in which the return of the tonic reinforces the tonal contrast in the manner of sonata form, but the ritornello idea falls by the wayside as the soloist performs seemingly improvisatory displays of embellishment techniques. These seemingly improvisatory displays recall the myriads of variation techniques developed by Tartini as part of his theory of ornamentation. Lombardini Sirmen's slow movements act as transitions from the first to the last movements, both of which are hardier movements, in a manner appreciated even by Mozart. Thus, in their intensity of expressivity, in their use of melodic variation through embellishment, and in their technical display, these middle movements link Lombardini Sirmen unmistakably to her Paduan heritage.

Finales: Lombardini Sirmen's reliance on third movement rondos should be considered within the time frame of the 1760s when rondo finales were still a new idea, with the exception of the finale of Concerto 4 which combines rondo and minuet forms. The finale of Concerto 1 is a seven-part ABA 'CA' 'DA''' structure in which the tutti and solo share in the statement of the rondo subject. The finale of Concerto 2 is a five-part ABA'CA'' structure having only one subject whose working out depends on a dialogue-like sharing of the two full statements of the subject over a remarkably broad tonic tonal plane. The finale of Concerto 3 breaks down into seven tutti solo sections plus cadenza, but the simplicity of the repeated thematic material—all in the tonic—is unusual. Bars 75–107 of the third solo section illustrate the composer's formulaic phrase structure where the material is arranged in groups of four and eight bar lengths. The last movement of Concerto 4 uses paired couplets, one of which is a 12-bar siciliano-like theme;

the other is a 24-bar minuet. The single moment of harmonic contrast here takes place in the second portion of the solo section. There is a total absence of the usual tutti-solo alternation since the tutti has just 24 bars. The formal layout of Concerto 4 becomes an ABAB ab ABA AB B rondo design. Concerto 5's finale is a nine-part structure, unless the ABA sections are interpreted as a rondo within a rondo or sonata rondo form, which is possible given the tonal transition to the dominant in A. The closing of Concerto 6 uses the seven part structure again with thematic statements shared by the tutti and solo. The two-part theme is spliced by a four-bar transition that represents the only use of transitional material in any of the six rondo movements.

Cadenzas: The cadenza, notationally indicated by the fermata and the tonic six-four chord, has been a distinctive feature of the solo concerto at least from Tartini's time. Tartini, in fact, is known to have written out some of his cadenzas. All but one of Lombardini Sirmen's 18 concerto movements have cadenzas indicated by the fermata and either a real or implied tonic six-four chord. In Concerto 4, the cadenza arrives on the penultimate chord, or, in other words, at a very late moment. The presence of the six-four chord, however, seems to guarantee that a cadenza was indeed intended by the composer. In general, cadenzas are placed very late to ensure release of tension at the very last. Preparation for cadenzas follows a regular pattern of unison or octave arpeggiation typical of style galant.

Harmony: Lombardini Sirmen's harmonic vocabulary is the typical one for the period. It includes augmented sixth cords, pivot chords in enharmonic modulations, and—rarely—the Neapolitan cord and deceptive cadence. Chromatic nuances appear quite frequently in an otherwise diatonic ambience. Her choice of keys extends from C (Concertos 4 and 6) to B flat (Concertos 1 and 5) to keys with three sharps (Concerto 3) and fours sharps (Concerto 2). There is no evident planned distribution of keys among the six works. All are in the major mode; all have the usual last movements in the same key and mode as the first and, except for Concerto 3, all have a middle movement in a contrasting key. The slow movement of no. 3 moves to the parallel mode; those of nos. 1 and 4 are in the dominant; those of nos. 2 and 5 are in the sub-dominant; and Concerto 6 uses the relative minor. Her interest in the minor mode would have been inherited from Tartini, whose emphasis on the need for expression is well established. The minor mode is explored significantly in the development sections of 16 of the 18 movements. Eleven of the movements follow the tonic-dominant-relative minor (I-V-vi-I) pattern; five use only the tonic major and/or minor plus dominant harmonies, and single movements use the sub-dominant tonality and the minor key—relative major to dominant tonal pattern.

Melody: There is little difference in Lombardini Sirmen's approach to melodic construction from one concerto to the next. The typically short motives, treated to alternating triadic and stepwise motion, resemble those of J.C. Bach and even Mozart and Haydn, although such style galant traits as triplets, circles around the tonic, arpeggiated closings, and repetition of themes an octave lower are also present. However, high notes, especially for the principal violin, are used strategically to give formal and dramatic intensity to several movements. This integration of sonority with larger consideration of melodic and structural design adds to the historical interest of Lombardini Sirmen's concertos. There is in these melodies both a promise of the pyrotechniques of Paganini and the Mozartean ideal of balance, symmetry, and interplay of soloist and ensemble. Probably the most advanced procedure is the return of thematic material from the exposition at the recapitulation at the same moment as the tonic tonality is re-established. The simultaneous return of themes and retransition to the tonic that delineates classic form is not fully achieved in Lombardini Sirmen's concertos, of course, since she relies on the abrupt change from her middle harmonies—usually the relative minor (vi)—to the tonic without making use of an harmonic transition. This abrupt return to the tonic with the recapitulation is a procedure that occurs throughout the set.

First Movements: The first movements have melodies of bravura character. Strongly accented movement combines with chordal and linear melodic outlines for main themes, more lyrical secondary themes, and transitional and closing ideas. There are instances in Concertos 1, 3, and 6 of new thematic material being introduced in the solo exposition either as transitions or as additional ideas stated in contrasting tonalities. True to the demands of sonata form, themes recur, although not with the completeness or regularity found in the authentic sonata allegro form.

The melodies of the first movements have piquant rhythms, chromatic interest, and even a vivaciousness that is not always to be found in those of her peers, even including J.C. Bach. Inevitably, though, these melodies tend to rely overmuch on dotted figures. Themes come in complementary sets of three (Principal, Secondary, and Closing) with transitions. Each of the sets includes themes that are syntactically, dynamically, and texturally contrasting. Principal themes are invariably eight bar units. They may be of the old-fashioned motivic web, as in the tutti exposition of Concerto 4 (bars 1–32), or of the two-bar motive reworked into an opening development section à la Haydn, as in Concerto 5. Secondary themes in some cases provide mood change. Closing themes have a special horizontal recitative cast that seems to offer contrast to the alternately rising and falling melodies—often over a two-octave ambitus—of the first two themes. The Mannheim-like syncoped, second beat cliché used by Stamitz *fils* and Haydn, among others, is a constant feature of Lombardini Sirmen's melodic cupboard. The use of anacrusis is another.

Opening tuttis function as dispensers of most of the melodies. All are closed, coming to a decided pause before the entry of the solo and usually acting as a fanfare for it. With the exception of Concerto 3, all of the solo sections in the exposition enter with the same thematic material as the tutti opened with. Themes are treated to genuine development by way of motivic rearrangement or transformation. Harmonic variation in one part of the central solo section contrasts with idiomatic figuration upon the themes in the second part of the central solo section. There is no set pattern for the use and reuse of given themes in developments. In Concerto 1, the main idea is the only thematic material in the entire development for both tutti and solo, while the second, closing, and transitional themes reappear in the recapitulation without the main idea. The composer's most unusual melodic device is the use of an introduction in Concerto 3 that reappears repeatedly to announce each new subject as it is stated throughout the movement.

Slow Movements: Themes in middle movements emphasise lyrical content even if they can be explained away as mere self-reproducing linear statements of the underlying harmony or melodies varied with ornamentation. A distinct theme and variation character (by way of embellishments) is noticeable in the through-composed, aria-like movements.

Finales. Rondo themes reveal an inclination towards the classic 36–bar idea, especially in Concerto 4 where the statement is 16 bars long and has a first part, a transitional theme, and a second part.

Rhythm: The rhythmic fabric of the concertos is post-Tartinian in its variety and complexity. Generally, various alterations of rhythm found in works up to 1760 as species of unwritten ornamentation are not a problem in Lombardini Sirmen's works. At least, based on available sources, graces would seem to have their time values correctly indicated. In Concertos 1–3, melodies veer through the up-and-down pitches in clusters of note values from eighths (quavers) to sixteenths (semi-quavers) to thirty-seconds (demi-semi-quavers), and in reverse order. In addition to a general slowing down of rhythmic textures in the last three concertos, the composer demonstrates her ability to move from one rhythm to another so that a feeling of transition rather than of sheer contrast prevails.

Most of Lombardini Sirmen's themes start incisively, intensify, then finish with a sudden slow-down at the cadence. A dominant trait is to finish a phrase with a fast turn around the tonic then to drop an octave. The anacrusis up-beats, syncopation including trills on weak beats, quarter-notes (crotchets) tied to eighths, triplets, and an instance of sextuplets, are other features. Rhythmic accents and contrasting points of articulation abound, although the engravers' and copyists' perseverance in notating these important signs is less than notable. The archaic braking formula still prevails in most conclusions of movement. As with her forays into experimental harmonic procedures, Lombardini Sirmen gives the horns in the first movements of Concerto 6 an unusual opportunity to preview a new rhythmic pattern that shortly afterward is given full play by the ensemble, but the procedure is never tried again. Not unexpectedly, dance rhythms—those of the gavotte, bourrée, and possibly the siciliano—can be found in the rondos.

Notes

1. Richard L. Crocker, *A History of Musical Style* (New York: McGraw-Hill, 1966), 355.
2. Donald F. Tovey, *Concertos*, vol. 3 of *Essays in Musical Analysis*, 7 vols. (London, 1944), 28.

Chapter 13

THE VIEWS OF POSTERITY

The earliest mention we have of Maddalena Lombardini Sirmen in a dictionary of music is from Germany. Ernst Ludwig Gerber in his *Historisch-Biographisches Lexikon der Tonkünstler* (Leipzig, 1790–92) wrote:

> Sirmen (Madam Maddalena Lombardini) was a very famous singer and virtuoso violinist, also a composer for this instrument. She was brought up in Venice at the Conservatorio of the Mendicanti as a singer, then became a violin pupil of the famous Tartini and was so successful as a violinist, especially in her interpretation of adagios, that she was put on a level with Tartini's best pupil, Nardini. In Mr Hiller's biography there is mentioned a letter from Tartini in which he teaches her about a number of ways of playing the violin. About 1782 she was a singer at the court of Dresden, but had previously made a number of concert tours where, especially in London, she was much acclaimed.

England was early on the scene with Abraham Rees' *The Cyclopaedia or Universal Dictionary of Arts, Sciences and Literature* (London, 1802–20). There was even an American edition. Rees, a London Presbyterian minister, had already brought out a new edition of Chambers' *Cyclopaedia* from 1779–86 when he embarked on yet another edition which was to appear in thirty-nine volumes between 1802 and 1820. Incredibly, Charles Burney between the ages of 75 and 79 wrote all the articles on music and even some of the more general ones. The piece on Sirmen is obviously lifted from his *History*.[1]

> SIRMAN, Mad. a celebrated performer on the violin, who had her musical education in a conservatorio in Venice. Her maiden name was Maddalena Lombardini. She was a favourite *élève* of Tartini, and it was for her that he drew up his little tract on the use of the bow on the violin, in the form of a letter "Arte dell'Arco". After quitting the conservatorio she married a German of the name of Sirman, and came to England in 1773, when her performance of Tartini's compositions on the violin was justly and universally admired. But in the operas of "Sofonisba" by Vento, and the "Cid" by Sacchini, she unadvisedly undertook the second woman's part on the stage, as a singer; but having been first woman so long upon the violin, she degraded herself by assuming a character, in which, though not deficient in voice or taste, she had no claim to superiority.

France soon followed in *Dictionnaire historique des musiciens, artistes et amateurs*, . . . by Alexandre E. Choron and F.J.M. Fayolle (Paris, 1810–11). This is almost an exact copy of Gerber but goes on to say that before Dresden, Maddalena had made many journeys to Paris and London. In 1824 John Sainsbury published his *Dictionary of Musicians from the Earliest Ages to the Present Time Comprising the Most Important Biographical Contents of the Works of Gerber, Choron, and Fayolle, Count Orloff, Dr Burney, Sir John Hawkins &c &c* (London). Sainsbury copied Gerber and Choron. And so it goes on through the nineteenth century with similar articles such as in F.J. Fétis's *Biographie Universelle des Musiciens* (Paris, 1864) and Hermann Mendel's, *Musikalisches Conversations-Lexikon* (Berlin, 1882). These articles are all factual and have the same basic information as Gerber.

In 1929 Walter Cobbett published his *Cyclopedia of Chamber Music* and M. Drake-Brockman wrote the article entitled "Women Composers". In it he says:

> One of the earliest known woman composers of chamber music was the violinist Maddalena SIRMEN (née Lombardini), b. 1735, a pupil of Tartini. Her works include

six string quartets (written in collaboration with her husband), six trios for 2 violins and 'cello (Welcker, London), and violin duets, as well as a number of so-called "concertos" for chamber combinations. Mr Alfred Moffat, well-known for his researches into the music of the past, has assured the writer that these works, though musicianly, have no remarkable features, and that they are not worthy of republication. The lady is chiefly known as the recipient of a famous letter touching on violin technique from Tartini, and "frequently quoted in modern works on the violin" (*Grove*).

Since at that time there were no scores of any of Maddalena's music in London—or anywhere else for that matter—and since it is unlikely that Moffat had the time or patience to put any of her music into score, he had probably never heard any.[2]

The first authoritative account of Maddalena's life was written by Olga Racster and E. Heron-Allen in the fifth edition of Grove's *Dictionary of Music and Musicians* (London, 1954). Olga Racster was actually Olga Rudge, the life-long secretary and companion of Ezra Pound, and was among the scholars responsible for the Vivaldi revival with her two articles published by the Accademia Chigiana, Siena, in 1939 and 1941. The Grove V article is quite long and well covers Maddalena's life as known in 1954. So I hope this present book will give a fuller and enriched insight into the life and background of an extraordinary talented lady; indeed, she really was "composer, violinist, and businesswoman".

Notes

1. There is an amusing account of the writing of the *Cyclopaedia* in *Scholes* II, 184–201.
2. Alfred Moffat (1866–1930) was an early researcher into seventeenth- and eighteenth-century English violin music.

Appendix A

LEOPOLD MOZART'S LETTER TO HIS WIFE AND SON

Salzburg, 12 April 1778

My dear wife and dear Son,[1]

Count Czernin is not content with fiddling at Court, and as he would like to do some conducting, he has collected an amateur orchestra who are to meet at Count Lodron's hall every Sunday after 3 o'clock. Count Sigmund Lodron came to invite Nannerl (as an amateur) to play the clavier and to ask me to keep the second violins in order. A week ago today, on the 5th, we had our first practice, there was Count Czernin, first violin, then Baron Babbius, Sigmund Lodron, young Wienrother, Kolb, Kolb's student from the Nonnberg, and a couple of young students whom I did not know. The second violins were myself, Sigmund Robinig, Cusetti, Count Altham, Cajetan Andretter, a student and Ceccarelli la coda dei secondi [the tail of the seconds]. The two violas were the two ex-Jesuits, Bullinger and Wishofer; the two oboes were Weiser, the lacquey, and Schulze's son, who acted in the Linz play. Two watchmen's apprentices played the horns. The double basses were Cassl and Count Wolfegg, with Ranftl doing duty occasionally. The cellos were the new young canons, Count Zeill and Spaur, Court Chancellor Mölke, Siegbert Andretter and Ranftl. Nannerl accompanied all the symphonies and she also accompanied Ceccarelli who sang an aria per l'apertura della accademia dilettanti [for the opening of the amateur concert]. After the symphony Count Czernin played a beautifully written concerto by Sirmen alla Brunetti, and dopo un altra synfonia Count Altham played a horrible trio . . .

Note

1.   Autograph in the Mozarteum, Salzburg.

Appendix B

TARTINI'S LETTER

[Translated by Barbara Graziosi]

Padua, 5 March 1760

My very much esteemed Signora Maddalena,

Finally, with God's will, I have finished with that weighty business which has prevented me from keeping my word to you; although I whole-heartedly wanted to. Let me assure you that my failing was entirely due to lack of time. I have started this letter in the name of the Lord, and I continue by begging you to write to me if my explanations are unclear and ask for clarification on all the points you do not understand.

The first and most important exercise and practice is aimed at perfecting all bowing technique; for you must have a good control of the bow whatever you play be it a rhythmic or melodic part.

The first point to which you must devote your attention is the contact between the bow and string. The bow should touch the string so lightly that the beginning of the note seems like the sound of someone breathing rather than a string being hit. The success of this first contact depends on keeping the wrist very flexible and continuing the movement without hesitation; for when the first contact is light there is no danger that the bowing will be rough or crude. You must be able to start this light bowing at all points in the bow: both in the middle and at both ends, leading the bow upwards and drawing it downwards. In order to save time, it is a good idea to start practising a crescendo on an open string, for example, the second, that is A. You must start pianissimo and increase the volume gradually to fortissimo, this exercise should be done both moving the bow up and drawing it down. Start with this exercise as soon as possible and practise it at least one hour every day, but at different times, you should practise a little in the morning and again in the evening. Please remember that this is the most important exercise of all and the most difficult.

Once you have mastered this exercise there is another type of crescendo which starts pianissimo, reaches fortissimo and dies down to pianissimo in one bow which would be easy for you. The first contact by you between bow and string will sound easy and confident and you will be able to make your bow do whatever you want.

In order to lighten your wrist, which is essential in order to play fast notes, it will be good for you to play some of Corelli's semi-quaver fugues every day. These fugues are three in number and belong to Op. 5 for violin solo. The first is to be found in the first sonata in D. You must gradually increase the speed at which you play them, until you reach the fastest pace you can manage. You should pay attention to two things while playing these fugues. In the first place, you must remember to play the notes *staccato*, that is, detached with a little rest between one note and the next. They are written like this:

but they must be played as follows:

Secondly, you should begin to play them with the point of the bow.
Once you feel confident with this, you should play them with that part
of the bow which lies between the point and the middle and when this
becomes easy, with the middle of the bow. You should also remember
to begin these fugues sometimes with an up-bow and sometimes with a
down-bow. By no means should you always start with a down-bow. In
order to acquire this light touch, it is also very useful to play fugues of
this type, in which you jump over the middle string.

You may play as many of these as you fancy, and in whatever key.
They are extremely useful, in fact they are vitally important.

As for the left hand, I have only one exercise to recommend, but I
think it is sufficient for a good command of the finger-board. Choose
any violin score, either the first or second violin part in a concerto, a
mass or song, anything will serve the purpose. Place your hand in the
half shift (second position), that is with the first finger on G on the first
string and play all the piece without moving your hand from that
situation unless you need to play A on the fourth string or D on the
first. In that case, once you have played them, you should move back to
the half shift (second position) without moving your hand down to the
natural (first position). Continue with this exercise until you are
confident that you can sight read in the half shift (second position) any
violin part, except those intended as solos. Then move up to the whole
shift (third position) and place your first finger on A on the first string
and repeat the exercise until you can play everything in the whole shift
(third position). When you feel ready, move your hand up to the double
shift (fourth position), with your first finger on B on the first string, and
when sure of that move to the fourth position of the hand making C
with the first finger on the first string. This is, as it were, a scale of
positions, and once you master it, you are in command of the finger
board. This exercise is absolutely necessary and I warmly recommend
it.

I now move on to the third exercise, which consists in playing trills. I would like you to be able to perform all these different trills because it is not true that one can play the same trill in slow and fast time. In order to practise two things at once, I suggest you start from an open string, either the first or the second, and play a crescendo. At the same time begin the trill at first very slowly, and then gradually, imperceptibly more quickly, until it is very fast. Perform it as shown in this example:

Do not follow this example literally, however, since here the demi-semi-quavers follow immediately on the semi-quavers which are twice as slow. Remember you want a gradation, not a leap. You should thus imagine other notes between semi-quavers and demi-semi-quavers which are shorter than the first and longer than the second. Those close to the semi-quavers should be almost as long as them, their duration should decrease rapidly as they move towards the demi-semi-quavers, until they become proper demi-semi-quavers. The same applies to the notes between the demi-semi-quavers and the next set of notes, which are double as quick. You should practise assiduously and devote your attention to this exercise. You should definitely start practising on an open string. Once you can perform a good trill on an open string, you will find that playing it with the second, third, and fourth finger is much easier. The fourth, or little finger, however, needs to be exercised more than the others since it is smaller than its brothers.

For the moment, I would not recommend any other exercises, these are more than enough if your zeal in practising them equals mine in recommending them. I hope you will let me know about your progress. For the time being, I send you my regards and beg you to pass them on, also to the Signora Priora [Fiorina Amorevoli], Signora Teresa [Bertoni], and Signora Chiara [Variati], I am their humble servant.

Please believe me, with greatest affection,

Your obedient and most humble servant,

Giuseppe Tartini

Appendix C

PUBLISHING HISTORY OF TARTINI'S "LETTER"

Compiled by Jane Baldauf-Berdes

1770   *L'Europa Letteraria* (Venice) 6–1–1770, V/II, 74–79

1770   *"Un importante lezione per i suonatori di violino"* (Venice, Paolo Colombani), (Bologna, Giovanni Battista Sassi), (Padua, Carlo Scappino)

1771   *A letter from the late Signor Tartini to Signora Maddalena Lombardini (now Signora Sirmen)* (London, Bremner), trans. C. Burney

1773   *"Lettre de Feu Tartini à Madame Magdeleine Lombardini . . ."* (Paris, *Journal de Musique*, no. 2)

1779   Burney trans. reprinted London

1783   *"Einige Gedanken Über Aufführung von Concertmusik"* (Hamburg, C.Fr. Cramer's Magazin der Musik I), trans. R. Bremner

1784   *"Brief des Joseph Tartini an Magdalena Lombardini"* (Leipzig, *Im verlage der Dykischen buch-handlung*), trans. Johann Adam Miller

1786   (Hanover, Pochwitz), trans. H.H. Rohrmann

1799   (Venice, Marescalchi)

1803   *"Tartini's Brief an Madame B***"* (Leipzig, *Allgemeine Musikali-sche Zeitung*, No. 9), trans. Johann Friedrich Rochlitz

1810   Included in *Notices sur Corelli, Tartini, Gaviniés et Viotti* (Paris, *Impr. littéraire et musicale*), trans. F.J.M. Fayolle

c. 1817 *L'Art de L'Archet ou Variations Composées par TARTINI . . . d'une Lettre de l'auteur adressée à Madame de Sirmen . . .* (Paris, Madame Joly), trans. Thomas

Appendix D

MADDALENA LOMBARDINI SIRMEN'S WILLS

Translated by Madeleine V. Constable

Venice, 9 June 1798

Death being certain, as too is the hour of its coming, I, Maddalena Laura Lombardini, daughter of the late Pietro and wife of Signor Lodovico Syrmen, think it advisable, since by God's grace, I enjoy perfect health, to dispose of what remains of my dowry, as specified in the inventory dated 16 September 1767, namely the sum of 110 ducats, with my husband's receipt of same attached thereto, as well as and including all my other earthly goods, for the most part acknowledged to be so by my husband, as also evidenced by various public documents, and this I do by this my will written in my own hand which I shall present by means of deeds drawn up by public notary, in order that my will be comprehensively executed after my death.

Firstly, with all my heart I ask the Almighty forgiveness for my many faults and beseech the Virgin Mary to intercede together with all the saints in heaven on my behalf, so that my soul may rejoice in the glory of heaven.

My funeral is to be conducted with a minimum of ceremony and the cost charged to my estate as it is at the time of my death, and should there be insufficient funds, my executor may utilize 150 ducats from the 2,000 ducats which I have invested with the nobleman Francesco Pisani of S. Stefano, this sum to serve for chantry masses for the repose of my soul.

In the first place, in disposing of my entire dowry as it appears from the above-mentioned inventory, and within the limits of the aforesaid sum, I establish as my heir my husband Signor Lodovico Syrmen at no inconvenience whatsoever to him; should my spouse die before the Rev. Giuseppe Terzi, I decree the aforesaid Rev. G. Terzi to be the heir of my estate and should both of them die, the beneficiary of my entire dowry is to be Alessandra my only child, wife of Sig. Francesco Leonardi.

Since my daughter has already received a dowry, and since she has been given as dowry a property which at the time of her marriage produced an annual rent of 110 scudi, and this to become effective in the case of the death of one of her parents, and in the meantime, having handed over to her clothing and linen, as appears in the inventory, besides my having given her from my own income, 40 Roman scudi per year, each worth 10 paoli, this to be continued each year until the aforesaid property is passed to her, and since it is my wish to benefit still further my daughter, that is following my death and that of my husband, and the death of Don G. Terzi, by means of the Fusconi acquisition, as also of half of the revenue from both the allotment [small-holding?] situated in Villa di S. Pietro in Vincoli, and likewise of that situated in another place known as the Argini, which was the last acquisition made together with my husband all of which are possessions in the territory of Ravenna, yet in order to pre-empt any unforeseen circumstances, since it is within my power to dispose of the aforesaid possessions, after my death and that of my husband and that of Don G. Terzi, should he survive us, it is my will that during his lifetime he be the beneficiary of the entirety, but after the death of both, I declare the beneficiary to be my aforesaid daughter Alessandra Leonardi, with the reservations mentioned earlier, namely that 15 scudi for 50 Masses per annum, each of 3 paoli, be said in the little church belonging to the Fusconi property, these Masses to be celebrated in perpetuity.

Regarding the remainder of my belongings, these being my own and resting apart from my dowry, for the sake of my peace of mind, since I feel it to be a duty, my wishes are as follows:

I wish the Rev. G. Terzi to have the use, during his lifetime, of the house owned by me and situated in Venice on the Fondamenta Nuovo, as it stands, also that he should likewise have the use, during his life-time of the sum of 2,000 ducats held by Francesco Pisani, with the exception of 150 ducats which I freely leave him, and of the 150 to be used, should the need arise, for my funeral expenses. On the death of Don Giuseppe, let the aforesaid capital sum be at once released, so that it may be distributed according to my final wishes, namely:

	ducats
I leave as a one-off payment to my husband a legacy of	200
Similarly to my daughter Alessandra Leonardi	100
to my sister Angela Lombardini Gottardi	50
to my sister's 3 daughters	50 ea
to Sig. F. Gottardi, my sister's husband	50
to Marina Terzi Campagnolo	50
to Marina's 3 daugthers	50
to Angela daughter of the late Bernardo Maddaleni (?),	500
my adopted daughter, to be invested in an annuity in her name	
to Donna Maria, the mother of the above named	100
Maddalena(?). Should Donna Maria be dead at the time,	
the aforesaid 100 to be added to the previously mentioned	
500 in favour of Angela	
to Nicola Syrmen, my husband's brother or to his family	50
to Don Raffaele Syrmen also my husband's brother	50
to the poor of the district of S. Giustina	50

The remainder of the capital is to be used forthwith for as many masses at 3 lire each for the repose of my soul and that of Don G. Terzi, distri-buted equally among the churches of my parish, that is the Capuccine church near my house, San Francesco della Vigna and S. Giovanni e Paolo and the Mendicanti.

Since Don G. Terzi has lived with me from the time of my marriage I wish that he may never be obliged by any person to be held to account for anything that may have belonged to me.

May all my clothing, linen and any other item, without exception, for the use or adornment of women, which I may have at the time of my death be passed entirely to Angela Maddalena, daughter of the late Bernardo, whom I adopted as my spiritual daughter, in the full realization of my duty to benefit her, not so much for her untiring care of me and of my house, as for the great love that she has borne me and for her continuous assistance, given out of a more than filial love and devotion, rather than from self interest, assuming that she continues to show me the same devotion and lives with me until my death.

All the furniture, household linen and other domestic items to be found in my house I wish to pass on to Don G. Terzi for his own use, without his needing to account for it to any person.

Upon the death of Don G. Terzi I likewise leave to Angela Maddalena, by way of a dowry my house with all the furniture, household linen etc. to be found at the time, without exception, and I wish that she not be held to account for it by any person, this being my will, since I feel in duty bound to benefit her in the aforesaid manner, so that she may not suffer after my death.

Should Don G. Terzi and Angela Maddalena think fit to do so, they may sell the house together with all the furniture considered superfluous in order to use the proceeds to the best advantage either by wise investment, or in the purchase of land, or in any other way, provided they are in agreement, and that my intentions are honoured, namely that this house, or the proceeds of the sale of it goes for the benefit of Don Giuseppe during his lifetime, and thereafter, serve for the maintenance of Angela Maddalena, my adopted daughter, on condition that she is with me at the time of my death and of that of Don G. Terzi.

To my executor I elect Sig. Antonio Baccalini, my neighbour, to assist at the time of my funeral, and similarly for any assistance required by Don G. Terzi and by Angela Maddalena, my adopted daughter, and I express this hope on the grounds of the good neighbourly relationship and friendship shown me during my lifetime; and may my executor be pleased to accept 15 ounces of silver which I leave him in memory, and similarly I leave 12 ounces of silver, or the equivalent, to my executor's wife, Sig[ra] Catterina Baccalini, praying that both of them may remember to have some Requiem masses said for the good of my soul.
Amen.

Signed: Maddalena Laura Lombardini, daughter of the
late Pietro, wife of Sig. Lodovico Syrmen

In the envelope, opened on 22 January 1983, containing the signatures of the two witnesses, Antonio Adami, son of Bortolo, and Giovanni Battista Pescatori, the following statement was found, drawn up by the notary Pietro Occioni, regarding Lombardini's handing over of the sealed package on 9 June 1798.

30 April 1806—Venice

Having made my will on 9 June 1798, and since from that time certain circumstances have changed, and since others may in time also change, and since I wish as far as I am able to remedy the slightest inconvenience, I declare by this my written codicil and signed by my own hand and in my own handwriting, that I confirm my Will, with the exception of those changes which I now make, namely as follows. The 50 ducats that I had intended to leave to Sig. Don R. Syrmen, my brother-in-law, and the other 50 ducats left to the poor of the district, forming a total of 100, I now leave to my servant Anna, daughter of Giacomo Ruffato, known as Pittoso, for whom I am concerned, as being the nearest poor person, and whom I feel in duty bound to acknowledge for the faithful and loving care shown to me; furthermore I leave her a bed with bed linen, and bedroom furniture, should she be in my service at the time of my death; and I leave my adopted daughter Angela Maddalena, she being my residuary legatee, to execute these dispositions, being certain that she will follow my wishes, many times expressed to her verbally.

Furthermore I commission as my executrix Angela Maddalena, my adopted daughter, in view of my changed circumstances, and since I have no more than a few items of silver which I have retained from the past to serve me in case of need, and since I am thus unable to show appreciation, as I had shown in my Will to my executor and to his wife, yet not wishing to cause trouble to any person without due compensation, I therefore wish absolutely that my sole executrix be my adopted daughter Angela Maddalena, and thus Sig. Antonio Baccalini, formerly appointed to be my executor will be exonerated; and since Angela Maddalena is the sole residuary legatee of that which remains, as expressed in my Will, for my greater peace of mind, and since I wish that she may not in any case or at any time be subjected to annoyance or disturbance, I take back my dowry from those in whose favour I had bequeathed it, and, as my final wish, declare that whatever I may possess in Venice, whether property or capital, or effects of any kind, all of this being of my own possession, be it land or assets not forming part of my dowry, or deriving from profits arising therefrom, and therefore constituting assets of which I may freely dispose, since none of this forms part of my dowry which, having been given to my husband, can never be recalled, neither can there be the smallest claim to whatever belonged to my husband, whether goods or property, and likewise neither to that which I possess or might have with me, in the case of my death; this much do I declare, for my enduring peace of mind, and from a sense of duty in the name of justice towards Angela Maddalena, my adopted daughter, she having spent her youth with me, toiling and assisting me in every way, and receiving no compensation in her lifetime. This therefore is my final irrevocable Will which I intend shall be faithfully carried out.

> I, Maddalena Laura Lombardini, daughter of the late Pietro,
> wife of Lodovico Syrmen affirm by my own hand.

[Venice, 15 September 1817]

I, Maddalena Laura Lombardini, widow of the late Lodovico Syrmen since 28 January 1812, my circumstances having changed through other critical situations, today annul and revoke all other dispositions expressed by Will and codicil, my intent being that this present Will, written and signed by mine own hand, be my final Will which at all times and in all contingencies must be fully executed.

Firstly, before the Almighty I ask fervently for forgiveness of my sins, imploring the valid assistance of Mary most holy and all the saints of Heaven, that my soul may rejoice in the glory of Heaven.

Although I was not satisfied with the testamentary dispositions made by my late husband, and similarly our only child Alessandra wife of Signor Francesco Leonardi believed that her interests were jeopardized by those dispositions, yet, for the sake of the deceased's eternal rest, and as a further token of my love for my daughter, I was persuaded to content her fully by renouncing at that time not only the use of property lately acquired by my late husband, which entitled me to have such use during my lifetime, but furthermore, by means of a gift between living [inter vivos], I gave over to her the Barbarelli acquisition, half of which belonged to me by virtue of the purchase contract, plus the other half since it formed part of my dowry, which I likewise gave up to her; moreover I passed to her my country property which was entirely my own, since it had been purchased with my own funds, so that, having made at that time such gifts, both from my dowry and apart from it, and now my assets being much reduced, and since it remains to me to fulfil my obligations towards Angela Maddalena, daughter of the late Bernardo, Angela having lived with me for 23 years as my adopted daughter and having given up her entire youth in my assistance, and in whose favour I should be duty bound offer some adequate support for the rest of her life, which I should have been able to do, had I not donated my country property, through the deed of gift to my daughter Alessandra, the use of which property might have been passed to my adopted daughter Angela Maddalena, as it would have been my duty to do; therefore being obliged to dispose of the present assets with uniformity, I dispose of my residual belongings as follows: my adopted daughter, Angela daughter of the late Bernardo I nominate my executrix, she being the one who is privy to all my affairs including my thoughts; when she has carried out my wishes in regard to my funeral and the payment of any debts I might have, and has given to the maidservant her bed and bedroom furniture which I have supplied to her during my lifetime, then, should I predecease Sig. Don G. Terzi, having left him all the contents of the 2 rooms used by him, i.e. the bedroom and the adjoining room, all of this being his own property without exception, and which he may freely dispose of without let or hindrance; thus once she carried out the above instructions without being answerable to any other person, this being my will, all that which remains, with no exceptions, my adopted daughter Angela, my executrix, shall share with my daughter Alessandra who, having had repeated evidence of the absence of self interest on the part of Angela and of Angela's love for her, particularly on the occasion of the deed of gift, will accept that portion of the remainder of my estate which will be allocated to her by my aforesaid executrix. I am certain that when I am gone, my daughter Alessandra will have the regard for and treatment of my adopted daughter Angela, which I myself have, as she, being the one who has sacrificed her entire life for me, fully deserves. I should have done much more for her, as I admit that the half of my remaining estate is poor recompense for that which she has suffered and done for me over so many years, bearing in mind that she has conducted herself with no ulterior motives of self interest. I trust she will not forget to pray for my soul for the rest of her days, as also, I hope my daughter Alessandra will do—Amen.

May God, in his mercy, concede to me eternal rest

M.L. Lombardini, widow of L. Syrmen

Venice 15 September 1817
                    Don Matteo
                    Antonio Combi witness

At the foot of the page in a different hand
                    Venice 18 May 1818
                    Registered at the office . . .
                    Giuseppe Linazzi (?)
Parish record of S.S. Giovanni e Paolo, Deaths [the same record as that of M.L. Syrmen, which follows]

On 6 May 1818 the Rev. Don G. Terzi, son of the late Gottardo and of Aurelia David, priest, native of Venice, resident in our parish on Fondamenta Nuove no. 3117, age 83 years, after 11 days of pleurisy/pneumonia, died at 3 a.m. Certified by Dr Gaetano Ruggieri (licence 101).

BIBLIOGRAPHY

Arnold, Denis, "Orphans and Ladies: the Venetian Conservatoires (1680–1790)", *Proceedings of the Royal Musical Association*, 89 (1962/63), 31–47.

——, "Music at the Mendicanti in the Eighteenth Century", *Music and Letters*, 65 (October 1984), 345–56.

Arnold, Elsie, "Maddalena Lombardini Sirmen compositrice, violinista e donna d'affari", in Vittoria Surian (ed.), *Gentildonne artiste intellettuali al tramonto della Serenissima* (Mirano, Venezia: Editrice Eidos, 1998), 117–26.

—— and Gloria Eive, "Maddalena Lombardini Sirmen", in Sylvia Glickman and Arthur Furman Schleifer (eds.), *Women Composers: Music through the Ages*, vol. 5 (New York: G.K. Hall, 1998), 388–424.

Baldauf-Berdes, Jane L., *Women Musicians of Venice: Musical Foundations, 1525–1855* (Oxford: Clarendon Press, 1993; rev. ed. 1996).

Bouquet, Marie-Thérèse, *Il Teatro di Corte dalle Origini al 1788* (Turin: Cassa di Risparmio, 1976).

Bouvet, Charles, *Une leçon de Giuseppe Tartini et une femme violoniste du XVIII siècle* (Paris, 1915).

Burney, Charles, *The Present State of Music in France and Italy, or the Journal of a Tour through Those Countries, Undertaken to Collect Materials for a General History of Music* (London: T. Becket & Co., 1774).

——, *A General History of Music from the Earliest Ages to the Present Period* (London: Becket; Robson; Robinson; Payne, 1776–89).

Burney, Charles, *The Present State of Music in France and Germany*, ed. by Percy Scholes (Oxford: Oxford University Press, 1959).

——, *A General History of Music from the Earliest Ages to the Present Period*, ed. by Frank Mercer (New York: Dover, 1935).

—— (trans.), *L'Europa Letteraria: Lettera del defonto signor Tartini alla signora Maddalena Lombardini inserviente ad una importante lezione per i suonatori di Violino* (London: Bremner, 1779).

——, *Music, Men, and Manners in France and Italy, 1770*, ed. by H. Edmund Poole (London: Eulenberg, 1974).

Constable, M.V., "The Venetian 'Figlie del Coro': Their Environment and Achievement", *Music and Letters*, 63 (July–October 1982), 181–212.

Fabbri, Giuseppe, Jolanda Scarpa, and Maria Carla Paolucci (eds.), *Arte e Musica all'Ospedaletto* (Venice: Stamperia di Venezia, 1978).

Fabbri, Paolo, *Tre Secoli di Musica a Ravenna* (Ravenna: Longo, 1983).

McVeigh, Simon, *Concert Life in London from Mozart to Haydn* (Cambridge: Cambridge University Press, 1993).

Mooser, R.A., *Annales de la musique et des musicians en Russie au XVIIe siècle* (Geneva: Mont-Blanc, 1948–51).

Petty, Frederick C., *Italian Opera in London, 1760–1800* (Ann Arbor: University of Michigan Press, 1980).

Pierre, Constant, *Histoire du Concert Spirituel, 1725–1790* (Paris: Société Française de Musicologie, 1975).

Piozzi, Hester Lynch, *Observations and Reflections*, ed. by Herbert Barrows (Ann Arbor: University of Michigan Press, 1967).

Scholes, Percy A., *The Great Dr Burney* (London: Oxford University Press, 1948).

Scott, Marion M., "Maddalena Lombardini: Madame Syrmen", in *Music and Letters*, xiv (1933), 149–63.

Selfridge-Field, Eleanor, *Pallade Veneta* (Venice: Fondazione Levi, 1985).

Tilmouth, Michael, "Music on the Travels of an English Merchant: Robert Bargrave (1628–61)", *Music and Letters*, 53 (1972), 143–59.

White, Chappell, "First-Movement Form in the Violin Concerto from Vivaldi to Viotti", in Thomas Noblitt (ed.), *Music East and West: Essays in Honour of Walter Kaufmann* (New York: Pendragon Press, 1981).

INDEX

163

ABOUT THE AUTHORS

Elsie Arnold was born in Liverpool, England, and is a music graduate of Sheffield University. Together with her late husband, Denis Arnold, she has spent a lifetime researching the music and musical institutions of Venice. Her publications include "Maddalena Lombardini Sirmen" , *The New Grove Dictionary of Music and Musicians*, ed. Stanley Sadie (2001); "Maddalena Lombardini Sirmen, Compositrice, Violinista e Donna d'Affari", ed. Vittoria Surian, Gentildonne Artiste Intellettuali al Tramonto della Serenissima (1998); with Gloria Eive, ed. Sylvia Glickman and Martha Furman Schleifer, "Maddalena Lombardini Sirmen", *Women Composers: Music through the Ages*, vol. 5 (1998); with Denis Arnold, *The Oratorio in Venice* (1986).

She lives in Oxford but spends as much time as possible at her house in the Veneto.

Jane Baldauf-Berdes received her B.A. in journalism from Marquette University, an M.M. in musicology from the University of Maryland, and a D.Phil. from Oxford University. Her publications include *Women Musicians of Venice: Musical Foundations, 1525–1855* (1993); *The Violin Concertos and Instrumental Chamber Music of Maddalena Laura Lombardini Sirmen* (1991); and other books and numerous articles and papers on Venetian music history and women musicians' studies.

At the time of her untimely death in 1993, she held the position of honorary fellow at the Women's Studies Research Center, University of

Wisconsin–Madison. She was also a member of the American Association of University Professors, American Musicological Association, Royal Musical Society, American Association for 18th Century Studies, British Scholars' Venetian Seminar, Early Music America, National Music Critics Association, and the British Society for Renaissance Studies.

Her extensive library on music in Venice and on the role of women in music history constitutes the Dr. Jane L. Baldauf-Berdes Archive for Women in Music at the Duke University Library.